Institutions
and
Organizations

W. Richard Scott

Institutions
and
Organizations

Foundations for
Organizational
Science
A Sage Publications Series

SAGE Publications
International Educational and Professional Publisher
Thousand Oaks   London   New Delhi

For information address:

SAGE Publications, Inc.
2455 Teller Road
Thousand Oaks, California 91320

SAGE Publications Ltd.
6 Bonhill Street
London EC2A 4PU
United Kingdom

SAGE Publications India Pvt. Ltd.
M-32 Market
Greater Kailash I
New Delhi 110 048 India

Printed in the United States of America

Library of Congress Cataloging-in-Publication Data

Scott, W. Richard
    Institutions and organizations / W. Richard Scott.
      p. cm. —(Foundations for organizational science)
    Includes bibliographical references (p.   ) and index.
      ISBN 0-8039-5652-5 (cloth : acid-free paper) . — ISBN 0-8039-5653-3
(pbk. : acid-free paper)
      1. Organizational sociology. 2. Social institutions. I. Title.
II. Series.
HM131.S3845 1995
302.3'5—dc20   95-10016

This book is printed on acid-free paper.

95 96 97 98 99 10 9 8 7 6 5 4 3 2 1

Sage Production Editor: Gillian Dickens

For Joy—
an altruistic agent who builds and sustains
institutions of value to many of us.

Contents

Preface

With the benefit of hindsight, I now can see clearly that from my earliest days I have been an institutionalist. My dissertation research, reported in Blau and Scott (1962), addressed the nature of professional work in an organizational setting. The question I pondered then was, if a concern for efficiency and productivity explains the nature of work systems, how is it that the same set of tasks can be conceived differently and be subject to different normative definitions and different performance criteria? Why is the same work viewed so differently by professional social workers than by bureaucratic administrators? Similar questions were pursued in my later research on authority systems (see Dornbusch and Scott 1975), where we examined differences among workers and between workers and supervisors in their "task conceptions" and explored the effect of these differences on the locus of discretion and the nature of the control systems developed. We discovered that organizational participants not only held different preferences for how work should be organized but also different levels of power, so that actual authority systems frequently diverged from preferences about such arrangements. And still later in my work on organizational effectiveness (Scott 1977), I asked who—

which stakeholders—had the right to set goals and standards and to sample work activities or outcomes, and I noted that the answer to these questions had profound effects on how organizations were structured and what was regarded as effective behavior.

One reason I came to these questions relatively early was because I tended to concentrate my research on professional organizations—organizations in which professionals share in the determination of goals and standards. Professionals differ from other classes of employees not only in the relative amount of power they exercise but in what aspects of work they attempt to control. As distinct from unions, professional occupations have sought to exercise control not only over the conditions of work (pay, benefits, and safety) but over the definition of the work itself. Professionals attempt to employ their power to shape the institutional frameworks supporting their activities in the broadest possible terms: They seek cognitive control—insisting that they are uniquely qualified to determine what types of problems fall under their jurisdiction and how these problems are to be categorized and processed; they seek normative control, determining who has the right to exercise authority over what decisions and actors in what situations; and they seek regulative control, determining what actions are to be prohibited and permitted and what sanctions are to be used (see Freidson 1986; Flood and Scott 1987; Abbott 1988; Scott and Backman 1990).

The explicit development of an institutional perspective in my own work, however, occurred only in association with my collaboration with John W. Meyer. For a number of years and with various colleagues, we pursued studies of teacher behavior as affected by school organization. Gradually, we began to realize that (1) schools are loosely coupled systems, so that apparently similar classrooms within the same school might be organized quite differently; (2) schools are open systems— teachers, classrooms, and schools are affected by the nature of their environments; and, in particular, (3) schools reflected in their internal structures the cultural beliefs and rules existing in the wider institutional environment. Meyer and Rowan (1977) produced the first systematic statement of the importance of institutional environments in shaping organizational structures to come out of this work. Later statements were produced by Meyer, Scott, and Deal (1981) and Meyer and Scott (1983b). (For a more detailed discussion of the origin of the institutional perspective in association with our research program in schools, see the preface to Meyer and Scott [1983b, pp. 7-17].)

In subsequent years, Meyer has pursued institutional arguments in association with others at the level of the world system (see Meyer and Hannan 1979; Thomas, Meyer, Ramirez, and Boli 1987; Meyer, Kamens, Benavot, Cha, and Wong 1992). And together, Meyer and I with various collaborators have attempted to expand and test institutional theory in further studies within educational settings but also by examining the diffusion of due process and fair employment practices and corporate training programs across diverse types of organizations (see Scott and Meyer 1994; Sutton, Dobbin, Meyer, and Scott 1994).

My own interests in institutional theory have led to me try to understand and relate intelligently to the work of others. Somewhat to my surprise, institutional theory has become, as my juniors would say, a hot topic. Work has developed, and at an accelerating pace, across a broad front and currently engages scholars in many disciplines associated with the study of organizations. In this book, I attempt to review and evaluate efforts under way in economics, political science, sociology, and, to a lesser extent, social psychology, as well as in organization studies. There is enough work, and it shows sufficient variety, that no brief review can do justice to all of the developments in this intellectual arena, but I have tried to incorporate its major strands.

I began the process of attempting to grasp institutional theory the year when I was a fellow at the Center for Advanced Study in the Behavioral Sciences (1989-1990). That halcyon setting encourages wider ranging scholarship and symbolizes the virtue of interdisciplinary inquiry. During that year, I drafted several articles all of which dealt with some aspect of institutional theory. Two of these (see Scott 1994b, 1994c) began the process of comparing and contrasting work on institutions across several disciplines. This book continues that effort.

Whom to thank, or blame, for my current understanding of institutional theory? My major debt is to John Meyer, my long-term colleague and collaborator, whose cognitive resources are both rich and subtle. I struggle to understand what he is talking about, and always find it worth the effort. For both intellectual stimulation and much-valued friendship, I will forever be grateful to Jim March. Other important local sources of friendship and intellectual challenge include Jim Baron, Mike Hannan, Jeff Pfeffer, and Bob Sutton, but also a wide assortment of stimulating colleagues associated with the Stanford Center for Organizations Research (SCOR). Also, several recent students (some of whom are now full-fledged colleagues) have helped to keep me honest and up to date. They include Andrew Creighton, Jerry Davis, Frank Dobbin, Stephen Mezias, Sue Monahan, David Strang, Mark Suchman, John Sutton, Ann Takata, Patricia Thornton, and Marc Ventresca.

Others not associated with Stanford have also been of great value to me as I pursued this work. I have benefited greatly from interacting in recent years with Paul DiMaggio, Neil Fligstein, Peter A. Hall, Richard Nelson, Walter Powell, Oliver Williamson, Mayer Zald, and Lynne Zucker. Also important have been connections to a set of Scandinavian colleagues who have challenged and contributed to my institutional learning. These include Nils Brunsson, Søren Christensen, Christian Knudsen, Helge Larsen, and Johan Olsen.

The editors for this series, particularly David Whetten and Andy Van de Ven, have been constructive and supportive in guiding this project, and I have benefited greatly from the suggestions and comments received from three colleagues who agreed to read an earlier draft of this work. My warm thanks to Christine Oliver, Jitendra Singh, and Marc Ventresca. I also received very helpful assistance from a current doctoral student, Peter Mendel, who reviewed an early draft. To a greater extent than most of us are willing to recognize, our individual scholarship is a social product.

Introduction

Institutional theory burst on the organizations scene during the mid-1970s and has generated much interest and attention (see Zucker 1988a; Powell and DiMaggio 1991). It has raised provocative questions about the world of organizations:

- Why do organizations of the same type, such as schools and hospitals, located in widely scattered locales, so closely resemble one another?
- How are we to regard behavior in organizational settings? Does it reflect the pursuit of rational interests and the exercise of conscious choice, or is behavior primarily shaped by conventions, routines, and habits?
- Why is it that the behavior of organizational participants is often observed to depart from the formal rules and stated goals of the organization?
- Why and how do laws, rules, and other types of regulative and normative systems arise? Do individuals voluntarily construct rule systems that then bind their own behavior?
- Where do interests come from? Do they stem from human nature, or are they culturally constructed?
- Why do specific structures and practices diffuse through a field of organizations in ways not predicted by the particular characteristics of adopting organizations?

- How do differences in cultural beliefs shape the nature and operation of organizations?
- Why do organizations and individuals conform to institutions? Is it because they are rewarded for doing so, because they think they are morally obliged to obey, or because they can conceive of no other way of behaving?

I see the ascendance of institutional theory as simply a continuation and extension of the intellectual revolution begun during the mid-1960s that introduced open systems conceptions into the study of organizations. Open systems theory transformed existing approaches by insisting on the importance of the wider context or environment as it constrains, shapes, and penetrates the organization (see Katz and Kahn 1978; Scott 1992, chap. 4). To the earlier emphasis on the importance of the technical environment—resources and technical know-how—institutional theory has called attention to the importance of the social and cultural environment, in particular, to social knowledge and cultural rule systems.

Much of the challenge of this subject—to the author as well as to the readers—resides in the many varying meanings and usages associated with the concept of institution. As one of the oldest and most often-employed ideas, it has continued to take on new and diverse meanings over time, much like barnacles on a ship's hull, without shedding the old.

I have two principal aims in this book. First, I hope to represent and review a great many of these disparate definitions; to describe the many meanings of the concept of institution and the usages to which it has been put. Chapter 1 reviews some of the principal views of economists, political scientists, and sociologists working at the turn of the century, a heyday of institutional activity. It appears that in this early period, institutionalists in economics operated primarily as gadflies and critics, on the margins of the discipline. By contrast, during this same time institutionalists were regarded as more mainstream in both political science and in sociology. Nevertheless, during most of the 20th century, as empiricism and positivism flourished, institutionalists in all disciplines were chased from center stage, persisting primarily in peripheral fields of study such as economic history, industrial relations, and the sociology of work.

At the time when the field of organizations was established as an academic specialty, at midcentury, institutionalists were hardly to be found. Chapter 2 relates the story of how institutional theory became connected to and developed within the area of organizations. It is important to recognize that although the early origins of institutional theory were in the disciplines, later contributions are being made not only by economists, political scientists, and sociologists but also by students of organization behavior and organization theory, management, and strategy.

Whereas these first chapters are primarily descriptive and arranged so as to provide a historical account, Chapter 3 reflects an analytic approach. It attempts to identify the core concerns and the principal dimensions around which the broader range of work on institutions and organizations has developed.

In addition to shifting from a historical to an analytic approach, Chapter 3 also provides a transition from my first aim—reflecting the diversity of work on institutions and organizations—to a second objective. I attempt to identify what is distinctive about the "new institutionalism" in organizational analysis. Although I discuss the new institutional work in the economics of organizations, my major interest is in explicating the sociological variant. I see this work as differing from earlier versions in two major ways: (1) It shifts attention from a primarily normative to a cognitive focus, and, more important, (2) it embraces a social constructionist rather than a social realist perspective. Briefly, although a normative view stresses social obligation as the basis for compliance, the cognitive view emphasizes the importance of how situations are framed and social identities defined. And although a social realist position begins with the assumption that reality is given "out there" in the world, a social constructionist position insists that reality is constructed by the human mind interacting in social situations. In short, in its more fully developed versions, the new sociological institutionalism differs from early forms not only in its conceptual focus but also in its ontological assumptions.

Chapters 4, 5, and 6 review and comment on empirical research relating to institutions and organizations. Chapter 4 describes research on the determinants of institutions, their persistence and their diffusion. Chapter 5 discusses research on the consequences of institutional structures and processes for societal systems, organizational fields, and organizational populations. And Chapter 6 reviews research on the consequences of institutions for organizational structures and processes. Surveying recent studies provides an opportunity to illustrate and further clarify differences in theoretical conceptions and assumptions underlying institutional research. Although a diverse body of literature is reviewed, I continue to give disproportionate time and attention to the sociological version of neo-institutional approaches to the study of organizations.

A concluding chapter, Chapter 7, summarizes the contributions made by institutional theory to our better understanding of organizations, reflects on unresolved controversies, and identifies what I believe to be promising new directions for future scholarship.

1 Early Institutionalists

No attempt will be made to provide a comprehensive or thorough review of early institutional theory, but to completely neglect this body of work would be a mistake. Although, as noted, much of this work is different from today's institutional efforts, a number of observers find the earlier work, in some respects, superior, and all contemporary work draws inspiration from the efforts of the pioneers. In examining this early work, it is well to recognize that contemporary students bring their own interests and agendas to the reading of these texts. As Alexander (1983a) observes: " 'Reading' is an important part of any theoretical strategy, and if the work in question is in any way open to varied interpretation then it certainly will be so interpreted" (p. 119). Conflicting interpretations are even more likely when the theorists in question change their views over time so that, for example, there appears to be an "early" Durkheim and a "late" one, or when, like Weber, they simultaneously express contradictory or ambivalent views.

Somewhat arbitrarily, I sort the work into disciplinary categories—as will soon become apparent, greater divisions often exist within than between disciplinary camps—and briefly review leading contributors to institutional thinking in economics, political science, and sociology.

1

Early Institutional Theory in Economics

It is well at the outset to acknowledge the lack of logical coherence in the strands of work to be examined. In many respects, the old institutional economics bears a stronger intellectual kinship to the new institutional approaches advanced by sociologists and anthropologists than to the new institutional economics. The earliest institutional arguments arose in Germany in the late 19th century as one byproduct of the famous *Methodenstreit*: the debate over scientific method. Drawing energy and inspiration from the earlier Romantic movement as well as from the ideas of Kant and Hegel, a collection of economists challenged the conventional canon that economics could be reduced to a set of universal laws. Led by Gustav Schmoller (1900-1904), this historical school insisted that economic processes operated within a social framework that was in turn shaped by a set of cultural and historical forces. Historical and comparative research was required to discern the distinctive properties of particular economic systems. Moreover, Schmoller and his associates called for economics to eschew its simplistic assumptions regarding "economic man" and embrace more realistic models of human behavior. The principal defender of the classical approach in this debate was Carl Menger (1871/1963), the Viennese economist, who insisted on the utility of simplifying assumptions and the value of developing economic principles that were both abstract and timeless (see Jaccoby 1988).

As with many intellectual debates, each warring faction sharpened and perfected its argument but both failed to convince one another. Attempts at reconciliation and synthesis occurred only among scholars of a later generation—principally, in the work of Weber and Schumpeter to be discussed later.

Many of the ideas of the historical school were embraced and further developed by American institutional economists, a number of whom had received training in Germany. An earlier cohort working in the mid-19th century did not receive much attention, but by the turn of the century, three institutional economists had become quite influential: Thorstein Veblen, John Commons, and Westley Mitchell. Although there were important differences in their views, all criticized conventional economic models for their unrealistic assumptions and inattention to historical change.

Veblen (1898) was highly critical of the underlying economic assumptions regarding individual behavior: He ridiculed "the hedonistic conception of man as that of a lightning calculator of pleasures and pains" (p. 389). By contrast, Veblen insisted that much behavior was governed by habit and convention. "Not only is the individual's conduct hedged about and directed by his habitual relations to his fellows in the group, but these relations, being of an institutional character, vary as the institutional scene varies" (Veblen 1909, p. 245). Indeed, Veblen (1919) defines institutions as "settled habits of thought common to the generality of man" (p. 239).

Commons similarly challenged the conventional emphasis on individual choice behavior, suggesting that a more appropriate unit of economic analysis was the "transaction," a concept borrowed from legal analysis. "The transaction is two or more wills giving, taking, persuading, coercing, defrauding, commanding, obeying, competing, governing in a world of scarcity, mechanisms and rules of conduct" (Commons 1924, p. 7). The "rules of conduct" to which Commons alludes are social institutions. Institutional rules were necessary to define the limits within which individuals and firms could pursue their objectives (Commons 1950/1970).

> To Commons, the institutions existing at a specific time represent nothing more than imperfect and pragmatic solutions to reconcile past conflicts; they are solutions that consist of a set of rights and duties, an authority for enforcing them, and some degree of adherence to collective norms of prudent reasonable behavior. (Van de Ven 1993, p. 142).

All three institutional economists emphasized the importance of change and were critical of their colleagues for not making its examination central to their mission. Veblen embraced an evolutionary perspective and insisted that a valid economics would emphasize the role of technological change and would trace the changing phases of the economy. Commons likewise stressed the centrality of change, viewing the economy as "a moving, changing process" (Commons 1924, p. 376). Mitchell believed that conventional economics was a hindrance to understanding the nature of the business cycle, and he devoted much of his energies to studying economic change. Like all institutionalists, he was reluctant to embrace an assumption of economic equilibrium. As one of the founders of the National Bureau of

Economic Research and chair of the committee that published the voluminous report *Recent Social Trends* (President's Research Committee on Social Trends 1933), Mitchell pioneered in the collection of empirical data on the operation of the economy, insisting that economic principles should be grounded in facts as opposed to abstract, deductive theories.

The American institutionalists were influenced not only by the German historical school but also by the homegrown philosophy of pragmatism as espoused by Dewey, James, and others. Their work reflected a suspicion of abstract, universal principles; an interest in solving practical problems; and an awareness of the role of chance events and historical contingencies (see Jaccoby 1988).

Jaccoby (1990) argues that the approaches offered by the early institutionalists departed from those adopted by their mainstream, neoclassical colleagues in four important respects:

Indeterminancy versus determinancy. Whereas the orthodox model assumed "perfect competition and unique equilibria, the institutionalists pointed to pervasive market power and to indeterminacy even under competition" (Jaccoby 1990, p. 318).

Endogenous versus exogenous determination of preferences. Neoclassical theorists posited individual preferences or wants, whereas institutionalists argued that such preferences were shaped by social institutions, whose operation should be the subject of economic analysis.

Behavioral realism versus simplifying assumptions. Institutional theorists argued that economists should use more pragmatic and psychologically realistic models of economic motivation rather than subscribe to naive utilitarian assumptions.

Diachronic versus synchronic analysis. Rather than assuming the "timeless and placeless" assumptions of the neoclassical theorists, institutionalists insisted that economists should ascertain "how the economy acquired its features and the conditions that cause these features to vary over time and place" (Jaccoby 1990, p. 320).

Whether or not they were correct in their accusations and assertions, the early institutional economists did not prevail: Neoclassical theory was victorious and continues its dominance up to the present time. Prior to the rise of the new institutional economics in the 1970s, only a few economists attempted to carry forward the institutionalist's agenda, the best known of whom are J. A. Schumpeter, John Kenneth Galbraith, and Gunnar Myrdal (see Swedberg 1991). Arguably, the subfields of economics most affected by the legacy of the institutional theorists are those of labor economics, the field in which Commons specialized; industrial relations, which focuses on broader social and political factors affecting economic structures and processes; and the economics of industry, which examines the varying configurations of industrial structures and their effects on the strategies and performance of individual firms.

Why was the impact of the early institutionalists blunted? Modern-day commentators offer several explanations. The German historical school no doubt overemphasized the uniqueness of economic systems and underemphasized the value of analytic theory. Even sympathetic critics acknowledge that Veblen exhibited "an explicit hostility to intellectual 'symmetry and system-building' " (Hodgson 1991, p. 211) and that Commons's arguments were hampered by his "idiosyncratic terminology and unsystematic style of reasoning" (Vanberg 1989, p. 343). But a more serious shortcoming was the tendency for the work to degenerate into naive empiricism. Emphasizing the importance of the particular, of time and place and historical circumstance, institutional analysis came more and more to underline "the value of largely descriptive work on the nature and function of politico-economic institutions" (Hodgson 1991, p. 211).

Here, then, we have the principal reason why the godfather of the new institutional economics, Ronald Coase (1983), so cavalierly dismissed the old institutional economics: "Without a theory they had nothing to pass on except a mass of descriptive material waiting for a theory, or a fire" (p. 230).

The battle between the particular and the general, between the temporal and the timeless, is one that contemporary institutional theorists continue to confront.

Early Institutional Theory in Political Science

Institutional approaches dominated political science in both Europe and America during the latter half of the 19th and the early decades of this century. I concentrate on the American scene. As carried out by such leading practitioners as J. W. Burgess (1902), Woodrow Wilson (1889), and W. W. Willoughby (1896, 1904), institutional analysis was grounded in constitutional law and moral philosophy. In the heavy tomes produced by these scholars, careful attention was given to the legal framework and administrative arrangements characterizing particular governance structures. Much of the work involved painstaking historical examination of the origins, controversies, and compromises producing specific regimes; some analyses were explicitly comparative, detailing how central problems or functions were variously managed by diverse governance mechanisms. But the underlying tone of the work was normative: "In the mainstream of political science, description was overshadowed by moral philosophy" (Simon 1991, p. 57).

As depicted by Bill and Hardgrave (1981), the institutional school that developed at the turn of the century exhibited several defining features. First, it was preoccupied with formal structures and legal systems. "Emphasis was placed upon the organized and evident institutions of government, and studies concentrated almost exclusively upon constitutions, cabinets, parliaments, courts, and bureaucracies" (p. 3).

Second, the approach emphasized detailed accounts of particular political systems, resulting in "configurative description"—intricate, descriptive accounts of interlinked rules, rights, and procedures (p. 3).

Third, the approach was conservative in the sense that it emphasized the "permanent and the unchanging." "Political institutions were examined in terms of an evolutionary development which found fulfillment in the immediate present. But while these institutions had a past, they apparently had no future" (p. 6). They were regarded as completed products.

Fourth, the work was largely nontheoretical, more attention being given to historical reconstruction of specific institutional forms. Finally, the tone of these studies was more that associated with moral philosophy and less that of empirical science. These scholars devoted more attention to the explication of normative principles than to the formulation of testable propositions.

Although he acknowledges many of the same characteristics, Eckstein (1963) also insists that these early institutionalists ushered in the first crude form of positivism in political science. Unlike their own predecessors, primarily "historicists" who focused their interest on abstracted political systems derived from philosophical principles, they were looking at the real world: at hard facts. Indeed,

> Primitive, unadulterated positivism insists upon hard facts, indubitable and incontrovertible facts, as well as facts that speak for themselves—and what facts of politics are harder, as well as more self-explanatory than the facts found in formal legal codes? (Eckstein 1963, p. 10)

In addition, these students were attending to the real world in yet another sense: They placed great emphasis on formal political institutions, on charters, legal codes, and administrative rules, in part simply because "the nineteenth century was a great age of constitution-making" (p. 10).

Beginning during the mid-1930s and continuing through the 1960s, the institutionalist perspective was challenged and largely supplanted by the behavioralist approach (not to be confused with "behaviorism" in psychology), which attempted to sever the tie to moral philosophy and rebuild political science as a theoretically guided, empirical science (see Easton 1965). More important for our concern, the behavioralist persuasion diverted attention away from institutional structures to political behavior.

> Behaviorists argued that, in order to understand politics and explain political outcomes, analysts should focus not on the formal attributes of government institutions but instead on informal distributions of power, attitudes and political behavior. (Thelen and Steinmo 1992, p. 4)

Students of politics focused attention on voting behavior, party formation, and public opinion. Moreover, this reductionist shift in emphasis from rules and structures to behavior was accompanied by a more utilitarian orientation, viewing action as "the product of calculated self-interest" and taking an instrumentalist view of politics, regarding the "allocation of resources as the central concern of political life" (March and Olsen 1984, p. 735). To study politics was to study "Who Gets What, When, and How?" (Lasswell 1936).

The new institutionalism in political science has developed in reaction to the excesses of the behavioralist revolution. Current institutionalists do not call for a return to "configurational history" but do seek to reestablish the importance of normative frameworks and rule systems in guiding, constraining, and empowering behavior. Moreover, it has come to be recognized that formal structures can exert important influences in social life apart from their effects on the behavior of those subject to them.

Early Institutional Theory in Sociology

Attention to institutions has been more constant in the sociological camp than that exhibited by either economists or political scientists. There are a number of different discernible strands with their distinctive vocabularies and emphases, but we also observe continuity from the early work of Cooley and Park through Hughes to the contemporary analyses of Freidson and Abbott; from the early efforts of Durkheim and Weber through Parsons to DiMaggio and Powell; from the early work on the social sources of mind and self in Mead and ideology in Mannheim to the emphasis on cognitive processes and knowledge systems in Berger and Luckmann and Meyer and Rowan.

Cooley and his followers emphasized the interdependence of individuals and institutions, of self and social structure. Although the great institutions—"language, government, the church, laws and customs of property and of the family"—appear to be independent and objective, they are developed and preserved through interactions among individuals and exist "as a habit of mind and of action, largely unconscious because [they are] largely common to all the group . . . . The individual is always cause as well as effect of the institution" (Cooley 1902/1956, pp. 313-314).

Hughes shared and developed this interdependent model. Deftly defining an institution as an "establishment of relative permanence of a distinctly social sort" (Hughes 1936, p. 180), he identifies their essential elements as

> (1) a set of mores or formal rules, or both, which can be fulfilled only by (2) people acting collectively, in established complementary capacities or offices. The first element represents consistency; the second concert or organization. (Hughes 1939, p. 297)

Although institutions represent continuity and persistence, they exist only to the extent that they are carried forward by individuals: "Institutions exist in the integrated and standardized behavior of individuals" (Hughes 1939, p. 319). In most of his writing, Hughes directed attention to the institutional structures surrounding and supporting work activities: in particular, to occupations and professions. His studies and essays are laced with insights on the myriad ways in which the institutional interacts with the individual—creating identities, shaping the life course ("careers"), providing a "license" to perform otherwise forbidden tasks and a rationale to account for the inevitable mistakes that occur when one is performing complex work (see Hughes 1958).

Empirical work developing these insights has focused more on occupations—in particular, professions—than on organizations as institutional systems constraining and empowering individual participants (see, e.g., Freidson 1970; Becker 1982; Abbott 1988). As a sociologist studying occupations, Abbott (1992) perceives an unbroken (Midwest/Chicago) tradition linking contemporary with earlier work and wonders what is so new about the new institutionalism in sociology. The institutional tradition has been carried forward in an uninterrupted fashion by the Chicago school of occupational research, but this is not the case for research on organizations. I believe that, over a substantial period during its development, the sociology of organizations largely lost sight of, defocalized, and gave insufficient attention to the institutional moorings of organizations.

The European tradition in institutional analysis was spearheaded by the two intellectual giants Émile Durkheim and Max Weber. The French sociologist Durkheim was preoccupied with understanding the changing bases of social order, but as previously noted, he appears to have modified his views over time. His classic *The Division of Labor in Society* (1893/1949) differentiated between the mechanical solidarity based on shared religious beliefs that integrated traditional societies and the newly emerging organic solidarity associated with an advanced division of labor. Initially, Durkheim viewed this new collective order as "based on the belief that action was rational and that order could be successfully negotiated in an individualistic way"— social order as "the unintended aggregate of individual self-interest" (Alexander 1983b, pp. 131, 134). But his revised arguments led him away from an instrumentalist, individualist explanation to focus on a collective normative framework that supplies "the noncontractual elements" of contract (Durkheim 1893/1949, book 1, chap. 7).

Durkheim's mature formulation emphasizes the all-important role played by symbolic systems—systems of belief and "collective representations" that, if not explicitly religious, have a religionlike character.

> There is something eternal in religion which is destined to survive all the particular symbols in which religious thought has successively enveloped itself. There can be no society which does not feel the need of upholding and reaffirming at regular intervals, the collective sentiments and the collective ideas which make its unity and its personality. (Durkheim 1912/ 1961, pp. 474-475)

These systems, although a product of human interaction, are experienced by individuals as objective. Although subjectively formed, they become "crystallized." They are, in Durkheim's (1901/1950) terms, "social facts": phenomena perceived by the individual as being both "external" (to that person) and "coercive" (backed by sanctions). And, as is the case with religious systems, ritual and ceremonies play a vital role in expressing and reinforcing belief. Rituals and ceremonies enact beliefs. They "act entirely upon the mind and upon it alone" (Durkheim 1912/1961, p. 420), so that to the extent that these activities have impact on situations, it is through their effects on beliefs about these situations.

These symbolic systems—systems of knowledge, belief, and "moral authority"—are for Durkheim social institutions.

> Institutions, Durkheim writes, are a product of joint activity and association, the effect of which is to "fix," to "institute" outside us certain initially subjective and individual ways of acting and judging. Institutions, then, are the "crystallizations" of Durkheim's earlier writing. (Alexander 1983a, p. 259)

The second major European figure contributing to institutional theory was Weber. As I will note in more detail in Chapter 2, more contemporary analysts of institutions lay claim to Weber as their guiding genius than to any other early theorist. Although Weber did not explicitly employ the concept of "institution," his work is permeated with a concern for understanding the ways in which cultural rules—ranging in nature from customary mores to legally defined constitutions or rule systems—define social structures and govern social behavior, including economic structures and behavior. For example, his justly famous typology of administrative systems—traditional, charismatic, and rational-legal—represent three types of authority systems differing primarily in the types of belief or cultural systems that legitimate the exercise of authority (see Weber 1924/1968, p. 215; Bendix 1960).

Although there remains much controversy as to how to characterize Weber's theoretical stance, this is largely because he stood at the crossroads of three major debates raging at the turn of the 19th century: first, that between those who viewed the social sciences as a natural science and those who argued that it was rather a cultural science; second, between idealist arguments associated with Durkheim and the materialist emphasis of Marx; and third, between the institutionalist historical school of economics and the classical interest in developing general theoretical principles. More so that any other figure of his time, he wrestled with and attempted to reconcile these apparently conflicting ideas.

Weber argued that the social sciences differ fundamentally from the natural sciences in that, in the former but not the latter, both the researcher and the object of study attach meaning to events. For Weber (1924/1968), action is social "when and in so far as the acting individual attaches a subjective meaning to his behavior" (p. 4). Individuals do not mechanically respond to stimuli; they first interpret them and then shape their response. Researchers cannot expect to understand social behavior without taking into account the meanings that mediate social action. Weber employed his interpretive approach to attempt a synthesis in which, although the material conditions and interests stressed by materialists such as Marx constrained choice and action, idealist interpretations of normative values—emphasized by Durkheim—motivated and activated action (see Alexander 1983b).

In developing his *Wirtschaftssoziologie* (economic sociology), Weber embraced the institutionalist arguments that economics needed to be historically informed and comparative in its approach, but at the same time he sided with Menger and the classicists in supporting the value of theoretical models that allowed one to abstract from specific, historically embedded systems to formulate and evaluate general arguments. Weber believed that economic sociology could bridge the chasm by attending to both historical circumstance and developing analytic theory (Swedberg 1991). Weber suggested that by abstracting from the specificity and complexity of concrete events, researchers could create "ideal types" to guide and inform comparative studies. If researchers were careful not to mistake the ideal types for reality—for example, to insist that individuals under all conditions would behave as economic men—such models could provide useful maps to guide analysis and increase understanding of the real world (Weber 1904-1918/1949).

The American sociologist Talcott Parsons also attempted to synthesize the arguments of major early theorists, in particular, Durkheim, Marx, Weber, and Freud, in constructing his voluntaristic theory of action (see Parsons 1937, 1951; Alexander 1983c).[1] Like Weber, he attempted to reconcile a subjective and an objective approach to social action by emphasizing that whereas normative frameworks existed independently of social actors, analysts needed to take into account the "orientation" of actors to them. A system of action was said to be "institutionalized" to the extent that actors in an ongoing relation oriented their actions to a common set of normative standards and value patterns. As such a normative system becomes internalized, "conformity with it becomes a need-disposition in the actor's own personality structure" (Parsons 1951, p. 37). In this sense, institutionalized action is motivated by "moral" rather than by instrumental concerns: "The primary motive for obedience to an institutional norm lies in the moral authority it exercises over the individual" (Parsons 1934/1990, p. 326). The actor conforms because of his or her belief in a value standard, not out of expediency.

Viewed more objectively, from the standpoint of the social analyst, institutions are appropriately seen as a system of norms that "regulate the relations of individuals to each other" and that define "what the relations of individuals ought to be" (Parsons 1934/1990, p. 327).

Contemporary theorists note several kinds of limitations with Parsons's formulation. Alexander (1983c) concludes that although Parsons attempted to develop a multidimensional view of social action, his conception of institutionalization put too much weight on cultural patterns, overemphasizing the "control exerted by values over conditions" (p. 242). The importance of interests and of instrumental action and rational choice was underemphasized. DiMaggio and Powell (1991) praise Parsons for the contribution he made to the "microfoundations" of institutional theory in his attempt to understand the ways in which cultural elements are incorporated by individuals. But they complain that his conception of culture failed to stress its existence as "an object of orientation existing outside the individual," viewing it instead as "an internalized element of the personality system"—giving too much weight to the subjective in contrast to the objective view. Additionally, they argue that Parsons's analysis of culture neglected its cognitive dimensions in favor of its evaluative components: culture as the internalization of "value-orientations" (DiMaggio and Powell 1991, p. 17). Each of these emphases drew Parsons away from examining the interaction of the instrumental and the normative in social action.

George Herbert Mead, like Cooley, emphasized the interdependence of self and society but gave particular attention to the role played by symbolic systems in creating both the human and the social. Meaning is created in interaction as gestures, particularly vocal gestures (language), call out the same response in self as in other, and self arises in interaction as an individual "takes on the attitudes of the other" in arriving at a self-conception (Mead 1934).

Stimulated by the work of Mead as well as by the contributions of Mannheim and Schutz, Berger and Luckmann (1967) redirected the sociology of knowledge away from its earlier concerns with epistemological issues or a focus on intellectual history to more appropriate sociological concerns, insisting that "the sociology of knowledge must concern itself with everything that passes for 'knowledge' in society" (p. 15). And this concern is not with the validity of this knowledge but with its production, with "the social creation of reality" (p. 15). Berger and Luckmann argue that social reality is a human construction, a product of social interaction. They underscore this position in their attention to language (systems of symbols) and cognition mediated by social processes as crucial to the ways in which actions are produced, repeated, and come to evoke stable, similar meanings in self and other. They define this process as one of *institutionalization.* In contrast to Durkheim and Parsons, Berger and Luckmann emphasized the creation of shared knowledge and belief systems rather than the production of rules and norms. Cognitive frameworks are stressed over normative systems. A focus on the centrality of cognitive systems forms the foundation for the sociological version of the new institutionalism in organizations.

Concluding Comment

This brief review has attempted to identify some of the varying interests and emphases of the early institutionalists, formulations developed between 1880 and the mid-20th century. As we will see, these theorists in numerous ways anticipated distinctions and insights later rediscovered by contemporary analysts. Nevertheless, most of this early work shared a common limitation: There is little attention to organizations. Some theorists focused their analyses on wider institutional structures, on constitutions and political systems, on language and legal systems, whereas others emphasized the emergence of common meanings and normative frameworks out of social interaction. Few, however, treated organizations themselves as institutional forms or directed attention to the ways in which wider institutions shaped intermediate organizing forms: organizational fields and organizational structures. Theorists in the 1950s and 1960s began to recognize the existence and importance of particular collectivities—individual organizations—that were distinguishable from both broader social institutions, on the one hand, and the behavior of individuals, on the other. Theoretical attention in the 1970s and 1980s to the significance of organizational fields—interorganizational systems exercising some controls over individual organizations but themselves linked to wider institutional frameworks—marks a development of similar import with relevance for current theory and empirical studies.

On reexamination, we observe much conflation of the concepts of institutions and organizations in the writings of Veblen and Commons, Burgess and Willoughby, Durkheim, Cooley, and Hughes. Perhaps Weber may be regarded as an exception to this generalization because, in much of his work, he was attentive to the effects of broader institutional forces in shaping and supporting differing administrative systems. But most of the early theorists folded together their notions of organizations and institutions. Only recently have theorists recognized the value of differentiating between these concepts.

Note

1. However, Camic (1992) argues that Parsons strategically selected these European predecessors—rather than American institutionalist scholars such as Veblen and Mitchell and his own

teachers (Hamilton and Ayres), who shared their interests—because of the tarnished reputation of these institutional economists at the time when Parsons was constructing his theory of action. There is a politics to selecting intellectual forebears that helps to explain why it is that some previous work is "drawn upon, while other work is overlooked" (p. 421).

Ironically, in a parallel fashion, R. H. Hall (1992) has accused sociological neo-institutionalists of failing to acknowledge Parsons (whose reputation until recently has been on the wane) as an important intellectual predecessor.

2 Institutional Theory
and Organizations

Early Applications to Organizations

Although, as we have seen, institutions were identified and analyzed quite early by social scientists, organizations, as distinctive types of social forms, were not distinguished conceptually until relatively recently. March (1965) dates the origins of organizational studies to the period 1937-1947, noting the appearance of the influential publications of Barnard (1938), Roethlisberger and Dickson (1939), and Gulick and Urwick (1937). These early efforts were reinforced by the translation into English of Weber's work on bureaucracy (1906-1924/1946, 1924/ 1947), which stimulated much interest among a collection of sociologists at Columbia, and by Simon's (1945/1957) work at the Carnegie Institute of Technology (now Carnegie Mellon University), including his important collaboration with March (March and Simon 1958). Parsons (1956/1960a, 1956/1960b) also became an early contributor when he was invited by James D. Thompson, the founding editor of *Administrative Science Quarterly,* a new interdisciplinary journal devoted to research on organizations, to prepare an article for the inaugural issue. Early and influential arguments linking institutions to organizations were associated with each of these developments.

The Columbia School and
Selznick's Institutional Model

Shortly after selections from Weber's seminal writings on bureaucracy were translated into English during the late 1940s, a group of scholars at Columbia University under the leadership of Robert K. Merton revived interest in bureaucracy and bureaucratization, its sources, and consequences for behavior in organizations (see Merton, Gray, Hockey, and Selvin 1952). It is generally acknowledged that a series of empirical studies of diverse organizations carried out by Merton's students—by Selznick (1949) of the Tennessee Valley Authority (TVA); Gouldner (1954) of a gypsum plant; Blau (1955) of a federal and state bureau; and Lipset, Trow, and Coleman (1956) of a union— helped to establish organizations as a distinctive arena of study (see Scott 1992, p. 9). What is less widely recognized is Merton's influence on Selznick's institutional theory of organizations.

As described below, Merton's (1936) early work on "unanticipated consequences of purposive action" was helpful to Selznick, but his analysis of bureaucratic behavior was even more directly influential. Although Merton (1940/1957) did not employ the term *institutionalization* in his well-known essay "Bureaucratic Structure and Personality," he provides a lucid discussion of processes within organizations that lead officials to orient their actions around the rules even "to the point where primary concern with conformity to the rules interferes with the achievement of the purposes of the organization" (p. 199). Merton depicts the multiple forces within bureaucracy producing discipline and orienting officials to a valued normative order. The strength of these pressures is such that officials are prone to follow the rules to the point of rigidity, formalism, even ritualism. Stimulated by the arguments of Durkheim and Hughes (and of Parsons), Merton (1940/1957) spells out his version of institutional processes within organizations:

There may ensue, in particular vocations and in particular types of organization, the process of sanctification . . . through sentiment-formation, emotional dependence upon bureaucratic symbols and status, and affective involvement in spheres of competence and authority, there develop pre-rogatives involving attitudes of moral legitimacy which are established as values in their own right, and are no longer viewed as merely technical means for expediting administration. (Merton 1957, p. 202)

Selznick's conception of institutional processes was strongly influenced by Merton's work. His views evolved through several of his writings. From the beginning, Selznick (1948) was intent on distinguishing between organizations as "the structural expression of rational action" (p. 25)—as a mechanistic instrument designed to achieve specified goals—and organizations viewed as an adaptive, organic system, affected by the social characteristics of its participants as well as by the varied pressures imposed by its environment. "Organizations," to a variable extent and over time, are transformed into "institutions." In his earliest formulation, Selznick borrows heavily from Merton's (1936) analysis of "the unanticipated consequences of purposive social action." Whereas some consequences of our actions occur as planned, others are unanticipated; social actions are not context free but are constrained and their outcomes are shaped by the setting in which they occur. Especially significant are the constraints on action that arise from "commitments enforced by institutionalization. . . . Because organizations are social systems, goals or procedures tend to achieve an established, value-impregnated status. We say that they become institutionalized" (Selznick 1949, pp. 256-257). In his later work on leadership, Selznick (1957) elaborates his views:

> Institutionalization is a process. It is something that happens to an organi-zation over time, reflecting the organization's own distinctive history, the people who have been in it, the groups it embodies and the vested interests they have created, and the way it has adapted to its environment.
>
>   In what is perhaps its most significant meaning, "to institutionalize" is to infuse with value beyond the technical requirements of the task at hand. (pp. 16-17)

As organizations become infused with value, they are no longer regarded as expendable tools; they develop a concern for self-mainte-nance. By taking on a distinctive set of values, the organization acquires a character structure, an identity. Maintaining the organization is no longer simply an instrumental matter of survival but becomes a struggle to preserve a set of unique values. A vital role of leadership, for Selznick, is to define and defend these values.

In addition to viewing institutionalization as a process, as something "that happens to the organization over time," Selznick also viewed institutionalization as a variable: Organizations with more precisely defined goals or with better developed technologies are less subject to institutionalization than those with diffuse goals and weak technologies (Selznick 1957).

Contrasting Selznick's with Merton's conception, both emphasized quite similar processes of value commitments to procedures extending beyond instrumental utilities. However, whereas Selznick focused on commitments distinctive to the developing character of a specific organization, Merton stressed commitments associated with characteristics of bureaucratic (rational-legal) organizations generally. Selznick's approach calls for depicting a "natural history" of the organization, a description of the processes by which, over time, an organization developed its distinctive structures, capabilities, and liabilities. He himself studied the evolution of the TVA, noting how its original structures and goals were transformed over time by the commitments of its participants and the requirements imposed by powerful constituencies in its environment (Selznick 1949; see also Chapter 4). His students conducted similar case studies of the transformation of organizations such as the Women's Christian Temperance Union (Gusfield 1955), a community college (Clark 1960), a voluntary hospital (Perrow 1961), and the YMCA (Zald and Denton 1963). In all of these studies, the official goals of the organization are shown to differ from—to mask—the "real" objectives that are transformed in interactions with interests both within and external to the organization. As Perrow (1986, p. 159) notes, Selznick's institutional school tends to produce an "exposé" view of organizations: Organizations are not the rational creatures they pretend to be, but are vehicles for embodying (sometimes surreptitious) values.

Another of Selznick's students, Arthur Stinchcombe (1968), has built on Selznick's formulation, making more explicit the role of power. Stinchcombe defines an institution as "a structure in which powerful people are committed to some value or interest" (p. 107), emphasizing that values are preserved and interests are protected only if those holding them retain power. Institutionalization connotes stability over time, and Stinchcombe's analysis attempts to identify the ways in which power holders are able to preserve their power, for example, by controlling the selection of their successors and general instruments of communication and socialization. He concludes: "By selection, socialization, controlling conditions of incumbency, and hero worship, succeeding generations of power-holders tend to regenerate the same institutions" (Stinchcombe 1968, p. 111).

Merton and Selznick laid the basis for a process model of institutions; Merton described processes operating in all or most bureaucratic organizations conducing officials toward overconformity, whereas Selznick focused on processes within particular organizations giving rise to a distinctive set of valued commitments. Stinchcombe elaborated the mechanisms used by powerful actors to perpetuate their interests and commitments.

Parsons's Institutional Approach

By contrast, in his analysis of institutional forces and organizations, Parsons develops his "cultural-institutional" arguments by examining the relation between an organization and its environment—the ways in which the value system of the organization is legitimated by its connections to "the main institutional patterns" in "different functional contexts" (1960a, p. 20). Although in most of his writing, as noted in Chapter 1, Parsons stressed the "subjective" dimension of institutions whereby individual actors internalize shared norms so that they become the basis for the individual's action, in his analysis of organizations, he shifts attention to what he terms the "objective" dimension: "a system of norms defining what the relations of individuals ought to be" (Parsons 1934/1990, p. 327).

Parsons argues that these wider normative structures serve to legitimate the existence of organizations but "more specifically, they legitimize the main functional patterns of operation which are necessary to implement the values" (1960a, p. 21). Schools receive legitimacy in a society to the extent that their goals are connected to wider cultural values, such as socialization and education, and to the extent that they conform in their structures and procedures to established "patterns of operation" specified for educational organizations. Note that in some respects this argument replicates at the organizational level Parsons's discussion of institutionalization at the individual level because it focuses on the individual unit's—whether a person's or an organization's—orientation to a normative system. Organizations operating in different functional sectors are legitimated by differing values, exhibit different adaptive patterns, and are governed by different codes and normative patterns. Moreover, value systems are stratified such that organizations serving more highly esteemed values are thought to be more legitimate and are expected to receive a disproportionate share of societal resources (Parsons 1953).

Parsons finds yet another use for the concept of institution. He argues that organizations tend to become differentiated vertically into three somewhat distinctive levels or layers: the technical, concerned with production activities; the managerial, concerned with control and coordination activities and with procurement of resources and disposal of products; and the institutional, concerned with relating the organization to the norms and conventions of the community and society. Every organization is a subsystem of "a wider social system which is the source of the 'meaning,' legitimation, or higher-level support which makes the implementation of the organization's goals possible" (Parsons 1960b, pp. 63-64). Parsons's typology of organizational levels was subsequently embraced by Thompson (1967) and has been widely employed. Moreover, in discussing the "points of articulation" between the three system levels, Parsons (1960b) notes that they are characterized by "a qualitative break in the simple continuity of line authority" because "the functions at each level are qualitatively different" (pp. 65-66). His discussion thus anticipates the recognition by later analysts of structural elements that are "loosely coupled" or "decoupled" (Weick 1976; Meyer and Rowan 1977).

Unlike Selznick's formulation, Parsons's theoretical work on organizations did not stimulate much empirical research. A few students, such as Georgopoulos (1972), employed Parsons's general conceptual scheme and described the importance of institutional underpinnings for specific types of organizations, but in general, Parsons's insights were not so much built on as rediscovered by later theorists.

The Carnegie School

Political scientist Herbert Simon developed his theory of administrative behavior to counteract and correct earlier theories that made heroic, unreasonable assumptions about rationality. Simon was among the first theorists to link the limits of individual cognitive capacity with the nature of organizational structure. In his classic *Administrative Behavior* (1945/1957), he described how organizational structures work to simplify and support decision making of individuals in organizations, allowing them to achieve higher levels of consistent and "boundedly rational" behavior than would otherwise be possible. In accepting organizational membership, individuals are expected to adopt organizational value premises as a guide for their decisions; factual premises—beliefs about means-ends connections—are also commonly supplied, in the form of organizational rules, procedures, and routines (Simon, 1957, pp. 220-247).

Together with March, Simon developed his arguments concerning the ways in which organizations shape the behavior of participants by developing routinized "performance programs" and recipes to follow when attempting to solve problems. March and Simon (1958) argue that, in many circumstances, "search and choice processes are very much abridged. . . . Most behavior, and particularly most behavior in organizations, is governed by performance programs" (pp. 141-142)— preset routines that provide guidance to individuals confronted by recurring demands. Such routines greatly reduce the discretion of most participants so that they both make fewer choices and are more circumscribed in the choices they do make. Value assumptions, cognitive frames, rules, and routines: These are the ingredients that conduce individuals to behave rationally. Indeed, "the rational individual is, and must be, an organized and institutionalized individual" (Simon 1957, p. 102). March and Simon's arguments, albeit among the earliest, remain among the most influential and clearest statements of the micro features and functions of institutional forms (see DiMaggio and Powell, 1991, pp. 15-26).

Cognitive Theory

Simon's work on behavior in organizations paralleled developments in social psychology, as this field of study—both its psychological and sociological sides—experienced the "cognitive revolution." During the 1940s and 1950s, the stimulus-response (S-R) approach began to be revised to include attention to the participation of an active organism (S-O-R) (see Lewin 1951). Early research concentrated on how the state of the organism, as defined by various motivational and emotional variables, affected perception, selective attention, and memory. Gradually, however, a concern with such "hot" cognition began to be superseded by attention to the effects of "cool" factors influencing everyday information-processing and problem-solving behaviors.

> The idea of the human organism as an information processor became popular. The mind came to be viewed by many as a computerlike apparatus that registered the incoming information and then subjected it to a variety of transformations before ordering a response. (Markus and Zajonc 1985, p. 141)

The question became, what types of "software" provided the programs and transformation rules for these processes?

The programs individuals use to select and process information are variously labeled *schemas, frames,* or *inferential sets.* These terms refer broadly to cognitive structures, ranging from "world views" to specific filing systems for classifying and ordering data (see Jones and Davis 1965; Neisser 1976). Extensive research by psychologists over the past three decades has shown that these cognitive frames enter into the full range of information-processing activities, from determining what information will receive attention, how it will be encoded, and how it will be retained, retrieved, and organized into memory to how it will be interpreted, thus affecting evaluations, judgments, predictions, and inferences (for an extensive review, see Markus and Zajonc 1985). In related work, Schank and Abelson (1977) introduced the concept of *script:* behavior patterns and sequences called up by specific roles or situations.

Psychologists have long vacillated between positions that regard individuals as basically competent, rational beings and views emphasizing cognitive biases and limitations. The general impact of recent cognitive theory and research has been to emphasize individual shortcomings as information processors and decision makers.[1]

Tversky and Kahneman (1974) pioneered in the identification of a number of specific types of biases likely to cause mistakes in assessing information and reaching conclusions. These and related problems were generalized by Nisbett and Ross (1980) into two common sources of inferential error: (1) a tendency to overuse simplistic strategies and to fail to employ the logical and statistical rules that guide scientific analysis and (2) a "tendency to attribute behavior exclusively to the actor's dispositions and to ignore powerful situational determinants of the behavior" (p. 31).

Even though their views have stressed the cognitive limitations of individuals, cognitive psychologists have recognized that individuals do participate actively in perceiving, interpreting, and making sense of their world. By contrast, until fairly recently, sociologists have tended to give primacy to the effects of structural factors, viewing individuals as more passive, conforming to the demands of their social systems and roles. "Identity theory" has emerged as a corrective to this over-socialized view, giving renewed attention to an active and reflexive self that creates, sustains, and changes social structures (see Rosenberg 1979; Stryker 1980; Burke and Reitzes 1981).

Identities are viewed as "shared social meanings that persons attribute to themselves in a role" (Burke and Reitzes 1991, p. 242). Such identities are socially produced by actors who locate themselves in social categories and interact with others in terms of these categories; they are "self-meanings" acquired in specific situations, and they are symbolically defined and reflexively managed (Burke and Reitzes 1981, 1991). By constructing and maintaining social identities, individuals construct personae that provide an individual and independent basis for action in social situations. In language developed by Giddens (1979, 1984), it helps to explain the basis for agency—individuals purposefully acting in pursuit of their interests—rather than meekly submitting to the constraints of the surrounding social structure.

Neo-Institutional Theory and Organizations: Founding Conceptions

We have arrived at the point in our history when the ideas that have come to be recognized as "neo-institutional" theory appeared. As we will see, in many ways they do not represent a sharp break with the past, although there are new emphases and insights. I begin by briefly reviewing the founding conceptions linking neo-institutional theory and organizations in economics, political science, and sociology. Then, in Chapter 3, I attempt a more analytic review of current theory, noting areas of consensus and dispute.

Neo-Institutional Theory in Economics

Neo-institutional economic theories are concerned with the rule and governance systems that develop to regulate or manage economic exchanges. These systems occur at many levels, including structures governing an entire economy and those exercising control over a specific industry as well as the administrative structures of individual organizations. Accounting for the emergence and change of entire economies has been of primary interest to economic historians (e.g., North 1990), industry systems have been examined by industrial economists (e.g., Stigler 1968), and studies of the sources of organizational forms are being conducted by a growing set of organizational economists. Although all of this work is properly regarded as institutional economics, it is the latter work, focusing on firm-level structures, which is especially identified with the new institutionalism in economics.

By consensus, the pioneer theorist inaugurating this new approach was Ronald Coase (1937), whose article "The Nature of the Firm" asks why some economic exchanges are carried out within firms under a governance structure involving rules and hierarchical enforcement mechanisms rather than being directly subject to the price mechanism in markets. Coase (1937) suggests that the reason must be that "there is a cost of using the price mechanism," namely, "the costs of negotiating and concluding a separate contract for each exchange transaction which takes place in a market" (p. 389). It is because of these "transaction costs" that firms arise.

This insight laid fallow—in Coase's (1972) own words, his article was "much cited and little used"—until it was resurrected in the 1970s by Oliver Williamson, who pursued its development by both "conditionalizing" and elaborating it. Williamson argues that transaction costs increase as a function of two paired conditions: when individual rationality, which is "bounded" (limited), is confronted by heightened complexity and uncertainty and when individual opportunism, which is always a possible threat, is coupled with the absence of alternative exchange partners. Under such conditions, exchanges are likely to be removed from the market and brought within an organizational framework or, if already inside an organization, to stimulate the development of more elaborate controls (Williamson 1975, 1985). He extends Coase's arguments by pushing them beyond the market versus firm comparison to consider a wide variety of "governance systems," ranging from markets to hybrid forms, such as franchising or alliance forms, to hierarchical forms, such as unified firms and multidivisional corporations (Williamson 1985, 1991).[2]

Thus the new institutional economics focuses primarily on the microanalytic questions of "the comparative efficacy with which alternative generic forms of governance—markets, hybrids, hierarchies— economize on transaction costs" rather than on the broader questions of origins and changes in the "institutional rules of the game: customs, laws, politics" (Williamson 1991, p. 269).

Neo-Institutional Theory in Political Science

As described in Chapter 1, neo-institutionalism in political science may be viewed, at least in part, as a reaction to the behavioralist emphasis that dominated the field at midcentury. However, the new institutionalists in political science and political sociology have grouped themselves into two quite distinct camps: the historical and the rational choice theorists.

The historical institutionalists, in many respects, hearken back to the turn-of-the-century institutional scholars who devoted themselves to the detailed analysis of regimes and governance mechanisms. Members of this camp include March and Olsen (1984, 1989), Hall (1986), and Skocpol (1985, 1992). Institutions are viewed as including "both formal structures and informal rules and procedures that structure conduct" (Thelen and Steinmo 1992, p. 2). These scholars emphasize that political institutions are not entirely derivative from other social structures, such as class, but have independent effects on social phenomena; that social arrangements are not only or even primarily the result of aggregating individual choices and actions; that many structures and outcomes are not those planned or intended, but the consequence of unanticipated and constrained choice; and that history is not usually "efficient"—a process "that moves rapidly to a unique solution" (March and Olsen 1984, p. 737)—but one that is much more indeterminate and context dependent.

The historical group takes a social-constructionist position that assumes "that capabilities and preferences, that is, the very nature of the actors, cannot be understood except as part of some larger institutional framework" (Krasner 1988, p. 72). Individual preferences are not stable and often result from rather than precede or determine choices. Institutions construct actors and define their available modes of action; they constrain behavior, but they also empower it. Analysis from this perspective is aimed at providing a detailed account of the specifics of institutional forms because they are expected to exert strong effects on individual behavior: structuring agendas, attention, preferences, and modes of acting.

These analysts attempt to show that political systems are not neutral arenas within which "external" interests compete, but rather complex forms that generate independent interests and advantages and whose procedures exert important effects on whatever business is being transacted. The structure of political systems, such as the state, matters (see Skocpol 1985). In accounting for the origins of these structures, the approach is primarily that of historical reconstruction. Although individuals build these structures, there is no assurance that they will produce what they intend. Current choices and possibilities are constrained and conditioned by past choices (see Skowronek 1982).

The second camp consists of the rational choice theorists and includes such scholars as Moe, Shepsle, and Weingast. These analysts view institutions as governance or rule systems, but argue that they represent rationally constructed edifices established by individuals seeking to promote or protect their interests. The approach represents an extension of the neo-institutional work in economics—including the transaction costs approach of Williamson and the work of agency theorists such as Alchian and Demsetz (1972)—to the study of political systems. Tullock (1976), an early advocate of importing economic models to explain political behavior, argues that "voters and customers are essentially the same people. Mr. Smith buys and votes; he is the same man in the supermarket and the voting booth" (p. 5; see also Buchanan and Tullock 1962). And Moe (1984) enumerates the major elements making up the paradigm adopted from the economists as including

> the contractual nature of organizations; markets vs. hierarchies, transactions costs, the rationality of structure, individualistic explanation, and economic methods of analysis. Standard neoclassical notions—optimization, marginality, equilibrium—are often central to work in this new tradition. (p. 750)

Political theorists recognize that economic models developed to account for economic organizations require modification if they are to
be applied to political systems. But they also insist that many of the
basic questions are parallel, including why do public organizations exist,
and how are we to account for their varying forms and governance
mechanisms? How can elected political officials, as principals, control
their bureaucratic agents? What are the effects of political institutions
on political and social behavior?

Rational choice theorists recognize that "in the reality of politics
social choices are not chaotic. They are quite stable." They are stable
because "of the distinctive role that institutions play." Thus the task
becomes to understand this role and, "more fundamentally, to determine where these institutions come from in the first place" (Moe
1990a, p. 216). The general argument embraced by these theorists is
that "economic organizations and institutions are explained in the
same way: they are structures that emerge and take the specific form
they do because they solve collective-action problems and thereby
facilitate gains from trade" (pp. 217-218).

Theorists disagree as to what is distinctive about political institutions. Weingast (1989) argues that politics differs from markets in that
in the former, actors cannot simply engage in market exchange but
must make decisions under some framework such as majority rule.
Shepsle (1989) suggests that the most important task of political
systems is to "get property rights right": to establish rule systems that
will promote efficient economic organizations. Moe (1990a) argues
that political decisions are distinctive in that they are "fundamentally
about the exercise of public authority" (p. 221), which entails access
to unique coercive powers. These and related researchers have attempted
to account for the distinctive powers of congressional committees
(Shepsle and Weingast 1987) and the inefficiency of governmental
bureaucracies (Moe 1990a, 1990b) as rational solutions to collective
problems.

Thus, whereas both political science camps share a view of the
importance of institutions in political life and share an interest in
attempting to account for the distinctive features of political institutions and in examining their effects on individual behavior, there are
few other commonalities. Historical institutionalists reject as unrealistic the rationality assumptions embraced by rational choice theorists.
The historical group regards the question of interests and preferences

as problematic and endogenous; the rational choice group takes interests as given and exogenous to the system being analyzed. Thelen and Steinmo (1992) amplify the historical theorist's stance:

> Historical institutionalists would not have trouble with the rational choice idea that political actors are acting strategically to achieve their ends. But clearly it is not very useful simply to leave it at that. We need a historically based analysis to tell us what they are trying to maximize and why they emphasize certain goals over others. (p. 9)

Finally, even given certain interests or goals, historical institutionalists emphasize the equifinality and multifinality of causation: The same interests may result in the creation of differing structures, and the same structures may result from different interests and choices.

Neo-Institutional Theory in Sociology

An important early attempt to introduce institutional arguments to the study of organizations was made by Silverman (1971), who proposes an "action" theory of organization. Silverman attacks prevailing models of organization, including contingency arguments and Parsons-Selznick's structural-functional views as being overly concerned with stability, order, and technical efficiency. Drawing on the work of Durkheim (1912/1961), Schutz (1962), Berger and Luckmann (1967), and Goffman (1961), Silverman proposes a phenomenological view of organizations, which focuses attention on meaning systems and the ways in which they are constructed and reconstructed in social action. Silverman (1971) contrasts his action approach with the prevailing "systems" view:

> The Systems approach tends to regard behaviour as a reflection of the characteristics of a social system containing a series of impersonal processes which are external to actors and constrain them. In emphasizing that action derives from the meanings that men attach to their own and each other's actions, the Action frame of references argues that man is constrained by the way in which he socially constructs his reality. (p. 141)

Drawing on the insights of Durkheim, Silverman argues that meanings operate not only in the minds of individuals but are also objective "social facts" residing in social institutions. The environments of organizations need to be conceptualized not only as a supply house of resources and target of outputs but also as a "source of meanings for the members of organisations" (p. 19).

Silverman's critique and attempted redirection of organizational theory had more impact in European than in U.S. circles (see Salaman 1978; Burrell and Morgan 1979). Moreover, in his subsequent work (see Silverman 1972; Silverman and Jones 1976), he shifts his focus to an ethnomethodological emphasis on the multiple meanings and rationalities associated with participants' phenomenological accounts of their common situation (see Reed 1985).

A subsequent effort to introduce institutional arguments into organizational sociology proved to be much more successful. Two influential articles appearing in the same year marked the arrival of neo-institutional theory in the sociological study of organizations. Articles by Meyer and Rowan (1977) and by Zucker (1977), like Silverman's work, build on Berger and Luckmann's (1967) conception of institutions. As discussed above, unlike the earlier institutional approaches developed by Merton, Selznick, and Parsons, which stressed the normative aspects of institutions, Berger and Luckmann emphasize the cognitive dimensions.

Meyer and Rowan embrace the view of institutions as complexes of cultural rules that were being increasingly rationalized through the actions of the professions, nation-states, and the mass media and that hence supported the development of more, and more types of, organizations. Organizations were not simply the product of increasing technical sophistication, as had long been argued, but also the result of the increasing rationalization of cultural rules, which provided an independent basis for constructing organizations. Meyer and Rowan emphasize the impact on organizational forms of changes in the wider institutional environment.

Whereas Meyer and Rowan develop the macro side of the argument, Zucker (a student of Meyer) emphasizes the microfoundations of institutions (see Zucker 1991). She stresses the power of cognitive beliefs to anchor behavior: "Social knowledge, once institutionalized exists as a fact, as part of objective reality, and can be transmitted directly on that basis" (Zucker 1977, p. 726).

Other influential contributions by DiMaggio and Powell (1983) and by Meyer and Scott (1983b) develop the macro (environmental) perspective, which has dominated sociological work. DiMaggio and Powell elaborate important mechanisms—coercive, mimetic, and normative—by which institutional effects are diffused through a field of organizations, and they emphasize structural isomorphism (similarity) as an important consequence of both competitive and institutional processes. And Meyer and Scott suggest that although all organizations are shaped by both technical and institutional forces, some types of organizations are more subject to one than the other. Both sets of authors identify the organizational field or sector as a new level of analysis particularly suited to the study of institutional processes.

There have also emerged in sociology investigators embracing a rational choice approach to social institutions. Their assumptions and approaches are quite similar to those already described as operating in economics and political science. Although their numbers and influence are considerably smaller in sociology, they include some prominent sociologists, such as Coleman (1990) and Hechter (1987; Hechter, Opp, and Wippler 1990).

Concluding Comment

Beginning in the early 1950s with the emergence of organizations as a recognized field of study, scholars began to connect institutional arguments to the structure and behavior of organizations. These institutional theories both built on and departed from the work of earlier institutional theorists.

Neo-institutional theory developed during the mid-1970s across the social sciences. In economics, this work departed substantially from the work of the early institutional economists by returning to a modified rational framework. In political science, two quite different schools have emerged, one building on the more historical approach of the early institutionalists and the other adopting and adapting economic neo-institutional models to the study of political structures. In sociology, the dominant approach has emphasized cognitive over normative frameworks and has focused attention on the effects of cultural belief systems operating in the environments of organizations rather than examining intraorganizational processes.

In the next chapter, I shift from a historical to an analytic approach. Beginning with an attempt to develop a more integrated model of institutions—drawing on contemporary work of the type just reviewed—I then identify several dimensions along which theorists differ as they consider the relation of institutions and organizations. I conclude by discussing two continuing bases of controversy.

Notes

1. It is to counteract such cognitive limitations that, according to March and Simon (Simon 1957; March and Simon 1958), organizations develop performance programs and decision-making routines.

2. A related line of theory and research, *agency theory,* also addresses the proper design of control structures to deal with the motivation and control of "agents"—those performing productive tasks—to ensure that they serve the interests of the "principal"—the person expected to be the prime beneficiary (see Alchian and Demsetz 1972; Jensen and Meckling 1976; Pratt and Zeckhauser 1985).

3 Contemporary Institutional Theory

Enough of history! Where does the area of institutional theory stand at this point in time? Can we make use of previous contributions to better understand the present situation and to chart future efforts? I begin with a broad definition of institutions that encompasses most contemporary views. Then I indicate where—around which issues and distinctions—the disagreements occur. The objective is not so much to achieve a consensus as to understand what the fighting is about. As it turns out, it is about important issues.

I begin with the following omnibus definition of institution: *Institutions consist of cognitive, normative, and regulative structures and activities that provide stability and meaning to social behavior. Institutions are transported by various carriers—cultures, structures, and routines—and they operate at multiple levels of jurisdiction.* In this conceptualization, institutions are multifaceted systems incorporating symbolic systems—cognitive constructions and normative rules—and regulative processes carried out through and shaping social behavior. Meaning systems, monitoring processes, and actions are

interwoven. Although constructed and maintained by individual actors, institutions assume the guise of an impersonal and objective
reality. Institutions ride on various conveyances and operate at multiple levels—from the world system to subunits of organizations.

Regulative systems, normative systems, and cognitive systems—all
of these elements have been identified by one or another social theorist
as vital components of institutions. One possible approach would be
to view each of these facets as contributing, in interdependent and
mutually reinforcing ways, to a powerful social framework—one that
encapsulates the celebrated strength and resilience of these structures. In such an integrated conception, institutions are viewed, as
D'Andrade (1984) observes, as overdetermined systems: "overdetermined in the sense that social sanctions plus pressure for conformity,
plus intrinsic direct reward, plus values, are all likely to act together
to give a particular meaning system its directive force" (p. 98).

Although there is value in such an inclusive model, there are also
disadvantages. This definition knits together three somewhat diver-
gent conceptions that need to be unpacked. Rather than pursuing the
development of this integrated conception,[1] I believe more progress
will be made at this juncture by distinguishing among the several
component elements and identifying their different underlying assumptions, mechanisms, and indicators.

Important differences exist among the various schools of institutional scholars. Although the most consequential dispute centers on
which elements are accorded priority, the disagreements have multiple
bases, centering around three axes of controversy. These are

- Varying emphases on institutional elements
- Varying carriers of institutional elements
- Varying levels of institutional elements

I consider each in turn.

Varying Emphases: The Three Pillars of Institutions

Rather than giving equal weight to the institutional elements—
regulative, normative, cognitive—various theorists have stressed one

Table 3.1 Varying Emphases: Three Pillars of Institutions

	Regulative	*Normative*	*Cognitive*
Basis of compliance	Expedience	Social obligation	Taken for granted
Mechanisms	Coercive	Normative	Mimetic
Logic	Instrumentality	Appropriateness	Orthodoxy
Indicators	Rules, laws, sanctions	Certification, accreditation	Prevalence, isomorphism
Basis of legitimacy	Legally sanctioned	Morally governed	Culturally supported, conceptually correct

or another as central, as is apparent from the review contained in Chapters 1 and 2. By employing a more analytical approach to these arguments, we can identify important underlying theoretical fault lines that transect the domain. Consider Table 3.1. The columns contain the three elements—three "pillars"—identified as making up or supporting institutions. The rows define some of the principal dimensions along which assumptions vary and arguments arise among theorists emphasizing one element over the others.

The Regulative Pillar

In the broadest sense, all scholars emphasize the regulative aspects of institutions: Institutions constrain and regularize behavior. Scholars supporting this pillar are distinguished by the prominence they give to explicit regulative processes—rule-setting, monitoring, and sanctioning activities. In this conception, regulative processes involve the capacity to establish rules, inspect or review others' conformity to them, and as necessary, manipulate sanctions—rewards or punishments—in an attempt to influence future behavior. These processes may operate through diffuse, informal mechanisms, involving folkways such as shaming or shunning activities, or they may be highly formalized and assigned to specific actors, such as the police or the courts.

Economists, including economic historians, are particularly likely to view institutions as resting primarily on the regulative pillar. The economic historian Douglass North, for example, features rule systems and enforcement mechanisms in his conceptualization.

> [Institutions] are perfectly analogous to the rules of the game in a competi-
> tive team sport. That is, they consist of formal written rules as well as
> typically unwritten codes of conduct that underlie and supplement formal
> rules . . . the rules and informal codes are sometimes violated and pun-
> ishment is enacted. Therefore, an essential part of the functioning of
> institutions is the costliness of ascertaining violations and the severity of
> punishment. (North 1990, p. 4)

This emphasis may stem in part from the character of their customary
objects of study. Economists are likely to focus their attention on the
behavior of individuals and firms in markets and other competitive
situations, where varying interests are more common and, hence,
explicit rules and referees are more necessary to preserving a stable
order. Economists see individuals and organizations as pursuing their
self-interests—as behaving instrumentally and expediently. The primary mechanism of control, employing DiMaggio and Powell's (1983)
typology, is coercion.

Force and fear and expedience are central ingredients of the regulative pillar, but they are tempered by the existence of rules, whether in
the guise of informal mores or formal rules and laws. As Weber (1968)
emphasized, few if any rulers are content to base their regime on force
alone; all attempt to cultivate a belief in its legitimacy. These beliefs,
however, may be relatively shallow, the actors merely acknow-
ledging the existence of the rule systems—recognizing the validity of
the rules—without necessarily believing that the rules are fair or
justified. Many individuals acknowledge the validity of the laws passed
by a duly constituted government without accepting their correctness,
their propriety (see Dornbusch and Scott 1975, pp. 38-40).

Recent work in economics emphasizes the costs of regulation.
Agency theory stresses the expense and difficulty entailed in accurately
monitoring performances relevant to contracts, whether implicit or
explicit (see Pratt and Zeckhauser 1985). Although in some situations
agreements can be monitored and enforced mutually by the parties
involved, in many circumstances it is necessary to invest the enforcement machinery in a third party expected to behave in a neutral
fashion. Economic historians view this as an important function of
the state. Thus North (1990) argues:

> Because ultimately a third party must always involve the state as a source
> of coercion, a theory of institutions also inevitably involves an analysis of

the political structure of a society and the degree to which that political structure provides a framework of effective enforcement. (p. 64)

North (1990, p. 54) also calls attention to problems that can arise because "enforcement is undertaken by agents whose own utility functions influence outcomes" (i.e., third parties who are not neutral). This interest is shared by political institutionalists, such as Skocpol (1985), who argue that the state develops its own interests and operates somewhat autonomously from other societal actors. In this and other ways, attention to the regulative aspects of institutions creates renewed interest in the role of the state: as rule maker, referee, and enforcer.

In many ways, this version of institutions is the most conventional, the most moderate one. It is consistent with a social realist perspective that presumes that actors have "natural" interests that they pursue rationally. This view of rationality emphasizes that individuals are instrumentally motivated to make their choices according to a utilitarian, cost-benefit logic. Analysts working within this framework struggle a bit to explain why it is that institutions emerge, as we will see, but once they are in place, they have no difficulty in explaining why rules are obeyed: It is in the actor's self-interest to conform. From this perspective, "norms and institutions affect the behavior of actors by altering benefit/cost calculations" (Hechter et al. 1990, p. 4). Actors behave expediently: They calculate rewards and penalties, whether these come from other individuals, from organizations, or from the state.

A stable system of rules backed by surveillance and sanctioning power is one prevailing view of institutions.

The Normative Pillar

A second group of theorists see institutions as primarily resting on a normative pillar (see Table 3.1). Emphasis here is placed on normative rules that introduce a prescriptive, evaluative, and obligatory dimension into social life. Normative systems include both *values* and *norms*. Values are conceptions of the preferred or the desirable together with the construction of standards to which existing structures or behavior can be compared and assessed. Norms specify how things should be done; they define legitimate means to pursue valued ends. Normative systems define goals or objectives (e.g., winning the game or making a profit) but also designate the appropriate ways to pursue them (e.g., conceptions of fair business practices).

Some values and norms are applicable to all members of the collectivity; others apply only to selected types of actors or positions. Such specialized values and norms are termed *roles:* conceptions of appropriate action for particular individuals or specified social positions. These conceptions are not simply anticipations or predictions but prescriptions—normative expectations—of what the actors are supposed to do. The expectations are held by other salient actors in the situation and so are experienced as external pressures by the focal actor. Also, and to varying degrees, they become internalized by the actor. Berger and Luckmann (1967) underline the centrality of roles for institutions: "All institutionalized conduct involves roles. Thus roles share in the controlling character of institutionalization. As soon as actors are typified as role performers, their conduct is ipso facto susceptible to enforcement" (p. 74). Roles can arise formally, as particular positions are defined to carry specified expectations for behavior, or informally, as over time through interaction differentiated expectations develop to guide behavior.

Normative rules are often regarded as imposing constraints on social behavior, and so they do. But at the same time, they empower and enable social action. They confer rights as well as responsibilities, privileges as well as duties, and licenses as well as mandates. In his essays on the professions, Hughes (1958) reminds us how much of the power and mystique associated with these roles comes from the license they are given to engage in "forbidden" or fateful activities—conducting intimate physical examinations or sentencing individuals to prison or to death.

The normative conception of institutions is embraced by most early sociologists—from Durkheim through Parsons and Selznick—perhaps because sociologists have tended to focus attention on institutions such as kinship or religious systems where common beliefs and values are more likely to exist. In this version of institutions, we begin to move away from a restricted definition of rational behavior. The normative approach to institutions emphasizes how values and normative frameworks structure choices. Rational action is always grounded in social context that specifies appropriate means to particular ends; action acquires its very reasonableness in terms of these social rules and guidelines for behavior. Here choices are structured by socially mediated values and normative frameworks. Actors conform not because it serves their individual interests, narrowly defined, but because it is expected of them; they are obliged to do so.

March's (1981; see also March and Olsen 1989; March 1994) distinction between the logic of instrumentalism and the logic of appropriateness helps to clarify the difference between a regulative and a normative conception of institutions. An instrumental logic asks, "What are my interests in this situation?" A logic of appropriateness asks, "Given my role in this situation, what is expected of me?"

March and Olsen (1989) develop a primarily normative conception of institutions:

> The proposition that organizations follow rules, that much of the behavior in an organization is specified by standard operating procedures, is a common one in the bureaucratic and organizational literature. . . . It can be extended to the institutions of politics. Much of the behavior we observe in political institutions reflects the routine way in which people do what they are supposed to do. (p. 21)

Although their conception of rules is quite broad, including "routines, procedures, conventions, roles, strategies, organizational forms, and technologies . . . beliefs, paradigms, codes, cultures, and knowledge that surround, support, elaborate, and contradicted those roles and routines" (p. 22)—their focus remains on social obligations:

> To describe behavior as driven by rules is to see action as a matching of a situation to the demands of a position. Rules define relationships among roles in terms of what an incumbent of one role owes to incumbents of other roles. (March and Olsen 1989, p. 23)

To view behavior as oriented to and governed by rules is not to suggest that behavior is unreasoned or automatic. March and Olsen insist that rules must be both selected (often more than one rule may be applicable) and interpreted: adapted to the demands of the particular situation. In related work, Searing (1991) argues that analysts emphasizing roles and rules need not view actors as slaves to social conventions but can see them as "reasonable people adapting to the rules of institutions." Roles can be viewed as "patterns, as configurations of goals, attitudes, and behaviors that are characteristic of people in particular situations" (Searing 1991, p. 1253).

Theorists embracing a normative conception of institutions emphasize the stabilizing influence of social beliefs and norms that are both internalized and imposed by others. For early normative theorists such as Parsons, shared norms and values were regarded as *the* basis of a stable social order. Institutional behavior is morally governed behavior. Later institutionalists emphasized the stabilizing effects of a different set of cultural rules: shared definitions of social reality. These views are championed by cognitive theorists.

The Cognitive Pillar

A third set of institutionalists, principally anthropologists like Geertz and sociologists such as Berger and Meyer and Zucker, stress the centrality of cognitive elements of institutions: the rules that constitute the nature of reality and the frames through which meaning is made (see Table 3.1). As DiMaggio and Powell (1991) correctly observe, a focus on the cognitive dimensions of institutions is the major distinguishing feature of the new institutionalism within sociology.

These institutionalists take seriously the cognitive dimensions of human existence: Mediating between the external world of stimuli and the response of the individual organism is a collection of internalized symbolic representations of the world. "In the cognitive paradigm, what a creature does is, in large part, a function of the creature's internal representation of its environment" (D'Andrade 1984, p. 88).

Symbols—words, signs, and gestures—have their effect by shaping the meanings we attribute to objects and activities. Meanings arise in interaction and are maintained—and transformed—as they are employed to make sense of the ongoing stream of happenings. Emphasizing the importance of symbols and meanings returns us to Weber's central premise. As noted in Chapter 1, Weber regarded social action as action to which subjective meaning is attached. To understand or explain any action, the analyst must take into account not only the objective conditions but the actor's subjective interpretation of them.

Social scientists have long recognized the importance of symbolic systems and shared meanings, but earlier work—for example, symbolic interactionism—treated such matters as primarily internalized and subjective. In keeping with the new work on culture (e.g., Geertz 1973; Douglas 1986; Rabinow and Sullivan 1987; Wuthnow, Hunter, Bergesen, and Kurzweil 1984), an important change embodied in neo-institutional theory in sociology is its treatment of symbolic systems and cultural rules as objective and external to individual actors. As I noted in Chapter 1, Berger and Luckmann (1967) were largely responsible for connecting this new work on culture to a conception of institutions. As summarized by Berger and Kellner (1981): "Every human institution is, as it were, a sedimentation of meanings or, to vary the image, a crystallization of meanings in objective form" (p. 31).

This is not at all inconsistent with an activist view of human actors. Individuals do construct and continuously negotiate social reality in everyday life, but they do so within the context of wider, preexisting cultural systems: symbolic frameworks, perceived to be both objective and external, that provide orientation and guidance (see Goffman 1974; Gonos 1977; Maines 1977; Swidler 1986; Zucker 1977).

And although a cognitive perspective directs us to give heightened attention to the symbolic aspects of social life, it would be a mistake not to attend also to the activities associated with these belief systems. Meanings arise in interaction, and they are preserved and modified by human behavior. To isolate meaning systems from their related behaviors is, as Geertz (1973) insists, to commit the error of

> locking cultural analysis away from its proper object, the informal logic of actual life. . . . Behavior must be attended to, and with some exactness, because it is through the flow of behavior—or, more precisely, social action—that cultural forms find articulation. . . . Whatever, or wherever, symbol systems in their own terms may be, we gain empirical access to them by inspecting events, not by arranging abstracted entities into unified patterns. (p. 17)

Similarly, for Berger and Luckmann (1967, p. 75) institutions are "dead" if they are only represented in verbal designations and in physical objects. All such representations are bereft of subjective reality "unless they are ongoingly 'brought to life' in actual human conduct."

A variety of cognitive elements can be identified (see D'Andrade 1984), but of foremost importance are *constitutive rules* (Searle 1969). These rules involve the creation of categories and the construction of typifications: processes by which "concrete and subjectively unique experiences . . . are ongoingly subsumed under general orders of meaning that are both objectively and subjectively real" (Berger and Luckmann 1967, p. 39). Such processes are variously applied to things, to ideas, to events, and to actors. Games provide a ready illustration. Constitutive rules construct the game of football as consisting of things such as goalposts and the gridiron, ideas such as winning and sportsmanship, and events such as first downs and offsides (see D'Andrade 1984). Similarly, other types of constitutive rules result in the social construction of actors and roles; in the football context, the creation of quarterbacks, coaches, and referees. Unlike the regulative view, cognitive theorists insist that games involve more than rules and enforcement mechanisms: They consist of socially constructed players endowed with differing capacities for action and parts to play.

Such processes, although most visible in games, are not limited to these more artificial situations. Because constitutive rules are so basic to social structure, so fundamental to social life, they are often overlooked. We take for granted that individual persons have interests and rights and capacities for action. It seems natural that there are citizens with opinions and interests, students with a capacity to learn, fathers with rights and responsibilities, and employees with aptitudes and grievances. But all of these types of actors—and a multitude of others—are social constructions; all depend for their existence on constitutive frameworks that emerged in interaction and are sustained and changed by ongoing interaction (see Berger and Luckmann 1967; Gergen and Davis 1985).

Moreover, recognition of the existence of such constitutive processes provides an explanation for much social behavior that differs greatly from lay interpretations or even from those found in much of social science. As Meyer, Boli, and Thomas (1987) argue:

> Most social theory takes actors (from individuals to states) and their actions as real, a priori, elements . . . [in contrast] we see the "existence" and characteristics of actors as socially constructed and highly problematic, and action as the enactment of broad institutional scripts rather than a matter of internally generated and autonomous choice, motivation and purpose. (p. 13)

In short, as constitutive rules are recognized, individual behavior is seen to often reflect external definitions rather than (or as a source of) internal intentions. The difference is nicely captured in the anecdote reported by Peter Hay (1993):

Gertrude Lawrence and Noel Coward were starring in one of the latter's plays when the production was honored with a royal visit. As Queen Elizabeth entered the Royal Box, the entire audience rose to its feet. Miss Lawrence, watching from the wings, murmured: "What an entrance!" Noel Coward, peeking on tip-toe behind her, added "What a part!" (p. 70)

The social construction of actors also defines what they see as their interests. As I have argued elsewhere:

Institutional frameworks define the ends and shape the means by which interests are determined and pursued. Institutional factors determine that actors in one type of setting, called firms, pursue profits; that actors in another setting, called agencies, seek larger budgets; that actors in a third setting, called political parties, seek votes; and that actors in an even stranger setting, research universities, pursue publications. (Scott 1987, p. 508)

Moreover, in some types of societal settings, it is regarded as natural that persons pursue idealistic or collectivist interests, whereas in others, individualist or materialist goals will be expected to dominate. Interests are not assumed to be natural or outside the scope of investigation: They are not treated as exogenous. Rather, they are recognized as varying by institutional context and as requiring explanation.

The social construction of actors is not limited to persons: Collective actors are similarly constituted and come in a wide variety of forms. Coleman (1974, 1990), for example, provides a useful historical account of the processes by which the limited liability corporation, an important contemporary collective actor, came into existence (Seavoy 1982; see also Creighton 1990), and Krasner (1988) has examined the circumstances under which nation-states came to be endowed with distinctive properties such as sovereignty. The development of such collective entities and the specification of their endowments, utilities, capabilities, and identities takes place over many years, but once established, they can serve as a cultural model for the molding of other similar forms.

The socially constructed characteristics of both persons and collective actors, such as firms, vary over time and place. Institutional rules in the West have accorded greater individual autonomy and independence to social actors—both persons and firms—than have related rules in Eastern societies. Thus, whereas "the United States has institutionalized competitive individualism in its market structure, Asian economies are organized through networks of [interdependent and less autonomous] economic actors that are believed to be natural and appropriate to economic development" (Biggart and Hamilton 1992, p. 472). Relations among persons or firms that the West views as collusion, the East sees as normal, inevitable, and beneficial.

The cognitive view insists that much of the coherence of social life is due to the creation of categories of social actors, both individual and collective, and associated ways of acting. We instantly recognize, feel comfortable in, and are able to take meaningful action is relation to such familiar collective actors as schools, hospitals, and restaurants. Rather than taking a realist view that such varied organizations are part of the natural order, theorists emphasizing this pillar regard the origin, maintenance, and diffusion of such forms as problematic—as requiring explanation. As students of organizations, our task becomes not simply to explain why one hospital is more effective than another, or why some schools exhibit more conflict than others, but to explain why some organizations are constituted as hospitals and others as schools. Where do these organizational templates come from, and how are they reproduced and transformed?

For cognitive theorists, compliance occurs in many circumstances because other types of behavior are inconceivable; routines are followed because they are taken for granted as "the way we do these things." Whereas the emphasis by normative theorists is on the power of roles—normative expectations guiding behavior—the cognitive framework stresses the importance of social identities: our conceptions of who we are and what ways of action make sense for us in a given situation. And rather than focusing on the constraining force of norms, cognitive theorists point to the importance of scripts: guidelines for sensemaking and choosing meaningful actions (see Schank and Abelson 1977; Lord and Kernan 1987).

Sociologists like Meyer and Rowan (1977) and DiMaggio and Powell (1983) emphasize the extent to which wider belief systems and cultural frames are imposed on or adopted by individual actors and organizations. Thus DiMaggio and Powell underline the extent to which organizations attempt to be isomorphic in their structures and activity pattern with specified cultural patterns present in their environments. The mechanism they identify that most clearly captures the cognitive dimension of isomorphic processes is imitation: mimetic processes. Individuals and organizations deal with uncertainty by imitating the ways of others whom we use as models. The underlying logic is often one of orthodoxy: We seek to behave in conventional ways, in ways that will not cause us to stand out or be noticed as different. Also involved are status processes. We attempt to imitate others whom we regard as superior, as more successful. One principal indicator of the strength of such mimetic processes is prevalence: the number of similar individuals or organizations exhibiting a given form or practice. Within fields of organizations, those performing similar tasks confront strong pressures for structural isomorphism.

By contrast, social psychologists are more likely to emphasize the interactive and negotiated nature of these choices. Constitutive rules need not simply be externally imposed on actors. Weick (1979, 1993), for example, emphasizes that understandings and scripts emerge out of actions as well as guide them and that collective symbols are as likely to be used to justify past behaviors as to guide current ones. These newer versions of role and identity theory emphasize that individuals play an active part, using existing rules and social resources to construct a social identity with some consistency across varying situations (see Burke and Reitzes 1991). Analysts have posited a "politics of identity" in which individuals or groups create goals, identities, and solidarities that provide meaning and generate ongoing social commitments (Aronowitz 1992; Calhoun 1991; Somers and Gibson forthcoming).

A cognitive conception of institutions stresses the central role played by the socially mediated construction of a common framework of meaning.[2]

The Three Pillars and Legitimacy

Each of the three pillars provides a basis for legitimacy, albeit a different one. In a resource-dependence or social exchange approach to organizations, legitimacy is sometimes treated as simply a different kind of resource. However, from an institutional perspective, legitimacy is not a commodity to be possessed or exchanged but a condition reflecting cultural alignment, normative support, or consonance with relevant rules or laws.

Berger and Luckmann (1967) describe legitimacy as evoking a "second order" of meaning (p. 92). In their early stages, institutions develop as repeated patterns of behavior that evoke shared meanings among the participants. The legitimation of this order involves connecting it to wider cognitive frames, norms, or rules. "Legitimation 'explains' the institutional order by ascribing cognitive validity to its objectivated meanings. Legitimation justifies the institutional order by giving a normative dignity to its practical imperatives" (Berger and Luckmann 1967, p. 93). Weber (1924/1968) argued that power became legitimated as authority to the extent that its exercise was backed by prevailing social norms, whether traditional, charismatic, or bureaucratic (see also Dornbusch and Scott 1975). And, more generally, Meyer and I argue that organizational legitimacy refers to the degree of cultural support for an organization (Meyer and Scott 1983a, p. 201).

This "vertical" dimension entails the support of significant others: various types of "authorities"—cultural as well as political—empowered to confer legitimacy. Who these are varies from time to time and place to place, but in our time, agents of the state and professional associations are often critical. Certification or accreditation by these bodies is frequently employed as an indicator of legitimacy. In complex situations, individuals or organizations may be confronted by competing sovereigns. Actors confronting conflicting demands and standards find it difficult to take action because conformity to one set of requirements undermines the normative support of other bodies. "The legitimacy of a given organization is negatively affected by the number of different authorities sovereign over it and by the diversity or inconsistency of their accounts of how it is to function" (Meyer and Scott 1983a, p. 202).

There is always the question as to whose assessments count in determining the legitimacy of a set of arrangements. Many structures diffuse because they are regarded as appropriate by entrenched authorities, even though their legitimacy is challenged by other, less powerful constituencies. Martin (1994), for example, notes that salary inequities between men and women are institutionalized in American society, even though the disadvantaged groups perceive them to be unjust and press for reforms. "Legitimate" structures may, nevertheless, be contested structures.

Stinchcombe asserts that, in the end, whose values define legitimacy is a matter of social power. He argues:

> A power is legitimate to the degree that, by virtue of the doctrines and norms by which it is justified, the power-holder can call upon sufficient other centers of power, as reserves in case of need, to make his power effective. (Stinchcombe 1968, p. 162)

The three pillars elicit three related but distinguishable bases of legitimacy (see Table 3.1). The regulative emphasis is on conformity to rules: Legitimate organizations are those established by and operating in accordance with relevant legal or quasi-legal requirements. A normative conception stresses a deeper, moral base for assessing legitimacy. Normative controls are much more likely to be internalized than are regulative controls, and the incentives for conformity are hence likely to include intrinsic as well as extrinsic rewards.

A cognitive view stresses the legitimacy that comes from adopting a common frame of reference or definition of the situation. To adopt an orthodox structure or identity in order to relate to a specific situation is to seek the legitimacy that comes from cognitive consistency. Hence, as the ecologists have proposed, prevalence or population density is a good indicator of the "taken for grantedness" of a social form or practice. (See Chapter 4.)

It is important to note that the three conceptions may lead to varying conclusions regarding the legitimacy of an organization. A regulative view would ascertain whether the organization is legally established and whether it is acting in accord with relevant laws and regulations. A normative orientation, stressing moral obligations, may countenance actions departing from "mere" legal requirements. Many professionals adhere to normative standards that compel them to depart from the rule-based requirements of bureaucratic organizations. And whistle-blowers claim that they are acting on the basis of a higher authority when they contest organizational rules or the orders of superiors. Street gangs may be highly prevalent in urban America, signifying that they provide a culturally constituted mode of organizing to achieve specified ends. Although we may readily recognize them, and their structures may be widely reproduced, they often are treated as illegal forms by police and other regulative bodies, and they frequently lack the normative endorsement of established community and societal authorities.

What is taken as evidence of legitimacy varies by which elements of institutions are featured.

Institutional Systems
Supporting Organizations

The institutional elements we have identified vary greatly in the substance or content contained in their rules, norms, or belief systems. Only a subset of these is conducive to the development and support of organizations. Numerous social theorists—from Weber to Parsons to Ellul to Berger to Meyer—have attempted to specify what types of institutional forms are likely to give rise to formal organizations.

Early views placed more emphasis on regulative structures. Weber (1924/ 1968, pp. 24, 953-954) stressed the emergence of a "legal order" consisting of a "system of consciously made rational rules" that support "instrumentally rational" action. Parsons (1951) devoted much attention in his work to detailing the value orientations and normative systems that would support the development of more instrumental and impersonal social forms. His development of the "pattern variables"—basic value dimensions giving rise to different kinds of action orientations and supporting structures—identified "universalism," "affective neutrality," "achievement," and "specificity" as normative orientations conducive to the rise of organizations.

Later theorists emphasized more cognitive dimensions supporting organizations. Ellul (1954/1964) describes the emergence of a "technicist" mentality that encourages analytic approaches and the development of systematic, instrumental rules to pursue specific objectives. Berger and colleagues (Berger, Berger, and Kellner 1973) describe the novel states of consciousness that accompany the emergence of technology and bureaucracy, including "mechanisticity," "reproducibility," "orderliness," and "predictability." And Meyer (1983, pp. 265-267) depicts the cultural elements that underlie the creation of formal organizations, including "definable purposes," "culturally defined means-ends relationships or technologies," conceiving of the world around organizations and the organizational participants as "resources," and presuming a "unified sovereign" that gives coherence to organizational functioning.

Meyer and colleagues (Meyer and Rowan 1977; Meyer and Scott 1983b) call attention to two rather different bases supporting formal organization. First, organizations grow up around technologically defined procedures that help to insure reliable performance. Second, organizations develop in relation to institutionalized beliefs ("rational myths") that specify means-ends relations in a rulelike manner that helps to ensure accountability (see also Hannan and Freeman 1984).

Social Stability

Every treatment of institutions emphasizes their contribution to social stability—that they are "establishment(s) of relative permanence" (Hughes 1936, p. 180). There is disagreement among theorists about the mechanisms producing stability. However, these disagreements do not appear to correlate closely with preferences for one or another pillar. Thus Jepperson (1991), who embraces a primarily cognitive approach to institutions, insists that the hallmark of an institution is its capacity for automatic maintenance, for self-restoration. Institutional mechanisms are those requiring no conscious mobilization of will or effort. But others sharing the cognitive perspective argue that the maintenance of institutions requires active effort. Thus DiMaggio (1988) scolds his colleagues for having too long neglected the role of power and agency in institutions and argues: "Institutional work is undertaken by actors with material or ideal interests in the persistence of the institution . . . : where such interests are not present and influential, deinstitutionalization occurs" (p. 13). I review other arguments regarding the basis of institutional stability in Chapter 4.

Assumptions Associated
With the Three Pillars

Although the differences among analysts emphasizing one or another element are partly a matter of substantive focus, they are also associated with more profound differences in underlying assumptions concerning the nature of reality and the logic of social action. As we have seen, theorists focusing on the regulative pillar are more likely to embrace a *social realist* ontology and a rational choice logic of action. Theorists emphasizing the cognitive pillar are more likely to work from a *social constructionist* set of assumptions and to take a broader view of social choice and action, embracing what DiMaggio and Powell (1991) term a "theory of practical action" (p. 22). Theorists stressing the normative pillar fall somewhere between these two camps, but closer to the cognitive than the regulative position.

Two related, but independent dimensions are at issue. First, there are differences in ontological assumptions, which pertain to how we understand the nature of what is real: whether the world around us is objective or is itself the product of social processes—of perceiving, categorizing, and naming. As Burrell and Morgan (1979) note, ontological assumptions

> concern the very essence of the phenomena under investigation . . . whether the "reality" to be investigated is external to the individual—imposing itself on individual consciousness from without—or the product of individual consciousness; . . . whether "reality" is a given "out there" in the world, or the product of one's mind. (p. 1)

Cognitive theorists, as noted, underline the critical importance of constitutive processes by which actors, both individual and collective, are constructed. To regard social actors as existing and acting independently of their social context is to reify them and to misspecify the nature of the forces at work. In the social constructionist view, individuals do not discover the world and its ways, but collectively invent them. Such invention is not random and arbitrary, but itself arises out of and is informed and constrained by existing social arrangements and beliefs.

By contrast, a social realist ontology presumes that actors are real— natural persons having innate capacities to act so as to secure and protect their interests. These interests are presumed to be inborn; they are taken as given. A regulative view presumes that actors are primarily responding to incentives and constraints operating in their environments. The environment too is regarded as real: it is out there as a part of the natural world.

Second, different assumptions are made regarding how actors make choices: what logics determine social action. As noted, a rational choice perspective assumes that actors behave expediently to pursue their preferences within a situation, although analysts in this camp vary considerably in terms of how restricted are the assumptions made regarding rationality. Game-theoretic analysts typically adhere rather closely to the lean, neoclassical formulation of the rational actor. Actors are presumed to have clear preference orderings, to be knowledgeable about the relation of alternatives to consequences, and to act so as to maximize their preferences (see, e.g., Axelrod 1984; Schotter 1981,

1986). By contrast, neo-institutional analysts in economics and rational choice theorists in political science usually begin with less restricted versions of rationality, usually Simon's model of bounded rationality that presumes that actors are "intendedly rational, but only limitedly so" (Simon 1957, p. xxiv; see also Abell forthcoming). These versions relax the assumptions regarding complete information and utility maximization as the criterion of choice (see, e.g., Williamson 1975; Moe 1990a). Regulative theorists are more likely to subscribe to some version of a rational choice theory of action.

Departing from these various models of rational choice, a varied group of contemporary theorists prefers to work with a broader and more socially embedded conception of the logic of social action. For analysts gathering under the normative pillar, choice is seen to be grounded in a social context and to be oriented by a moral dimension that takes into account one's relations and obligations to others in the situation. A logic of appropriateness replaces, or sets limits on, instrumental behavior.

Cognitive theorists emphasize the extent to which choice is informed and constrained by the ways in which knowledge is constructed. The social construction of reality is seen as ongoing, continuously, at macro-, meso-, and micro-levels. At the broadest levels, science, the professions, and the mass media operate to create new categories, typifications, and causal connections. At the intermediate levels, individuals operate within particular social arenas, such as educational, work, and family settings, which carry with them many codified cultural rules and social routines. And in everyday interaction, at the microlevel, individuals appropriate and employ these broader cultural frameworks but also improvise and invent new understandings and interpretations that guide their daily activities. Individuals are not simply constrained but informed and empowered by these preexisting knowledge and rule systems.

Broad cultural beliefs as well as individual self-conceptions are the product of social processes. The identities of actors and their interests are viewed as resulting from these forces. Preferences are not taken as given: They are not "exogenous" to the analysis, but among the most important factors to be explained. Both ends and means are institutionally shaped. More important, individuals in interaction collectively construct the social world—including individual and collective

Table 3.2   Institutional Pillars and Carriers

| | Pillar | | |
Carrier	Regulative	Normative	Cognitive
Cultures	Rules, laws	Values, expectations	Categories, typifications
Social structures	Governance systems, power systems	Regimes, authority systems	Structural isomorphism, identities
Routines	Protocols, standard procedures	Conformity, performance of duty	Performance programs, scripts

economic actors and their interests. Economic actors and relations are not simply embedded in social structures: They *are* social structures.

In sum, contemporary theorists not only select different pillars to support their versions of institutional structure; these pillars themselves rest on fundamentally different assumptions regarding the nature of reality and how to account for behavior.

Varying Carriers

Institutions, whether regulative, normative, or cognitive perspectives are stressed, are embedded in various types of repositories or "carriers." In his analysis of institutions, Jepperson (1991, p. 150) identifies three types of carriers: cultures, regimes, and organizations. I propose a somewhat revised set: *cultures, social structures,* and *routines.* These distinctions are orthogonal to the three elements or pillars just described, permitting us to cross-classify them (see Table 3.2). Theorists vary not only in which elements they favor, but in which carriers they emphasize.

In developing the concept of carrier, I draw not only on Jepperson's work as noted, but also on Giddens's (1984) theory of structuration that emphasizes the reciprocal relation of structure and action in all social behavior.[3] In Giddens's formulation, structure represents the persistent or more institutionalized aspect of behavior. Structures are both the result of past actions—social products—as well as the context or medium within which ongoing action occurs. For its part, action operates to produce—to reproduce (perpetuate) or alter—structure. Each of the three carriers is viewed as involving structure and action, but identifies three different subtypes of structure.

Cultural Carriers

Cultures are carriers that rely primarily on interpretive structures—on codified patterns of meanings and rule systems. Such interpretive schemes inform and constrain ongoing behavior but are also reinforced and changed by these behaviors. These rule systems may exist in the wider environment at the societal or even world system levels, or they may be more restricted in their jurisdiction, applying only to specific organizational fields or organizations, as I discuss below.

As the entries in Table 3.2 suggest, the aspects of culture emphasized vary depending on which elements of institutions are given prominence. Cognitive theorists will stress the importance of categories, distinctions, and typifications; normative theorists will accent shared values and normative expectations; and regulative theorists, conventions, rules, and laws.

Some types of cultural beliefs will be specific to a given organization or one of its subsystems, giving rise to a corporate culture (see Frost, Moore, Louis, Lundberg, and Martin 1991). Other cultural systems will operate at a more general level, consisting of belief systems that are transorganizational and may be quite widespread. Although it is conventional to characterize such systems as operating in the organization's environment (see Meyer and Scott 1983b; Zucker 1987), it is important to recognize that cultural beliefs are carried in the minds of individuals. They exist not only in the wider environment as widely held beliefs or as laws that organizational actors need to take into account but also as ideas or values in the heads of organizational actors.

Bourdieu (1977), in particular, emphasizes the internalization of cultural rules. His concept of *habitus* refers to the existence of a "system of lasting and transposable dispositions which, integrating past experiences, functions at every moment as a matrix of perceptions, appreciations and actions," allowing individuals to structure their behavior within situations.

Social Structural Carriers

Institutions can also be carried by social structures. Social structures are carriers that rely on patterned expectations connected to networks of social positions: role systems. Again, the structures constrain and

empower the behavior of actors at the same time that they are reproduced and transformed by this behavior.

Rules and belief systems are coded into structural distinctions and
roles; structures incorporate—instantiate—institutional elements. As
with cultural carriers, some structural forms are widely shared across
many organizations, creating structural isomorphism (similar forms) or
structural equivalence (similar relations among forms). Other forms
may be distinctive to a particular organization, embodying localized
belief systems and creating what Selznick (1957) termed a unique
organizational "character structure."

As with cultures, the aspects of structure emphasized depend on which
elements of institutions are featured. Cognitive theorists stress structural
isomorphism. Cognitive typifications are often coded into organizational structures as differentiated departments and roles. For example,
codified knowledge systems support the development of differentiated
academic departments in universities. Normative and regulative theorists are apt to view structures as governance systems, emphasizing
either the normative (authority) or the coercive (power) aspects of
these structures.[4] Such governance systems are viewed as creating and
enforcing codes, norms, and rules and as monitoring and sanctioning
the activities of participants. The new institutional economists, such
as Williamson, emphasize structures erected to exercise governance as
the principal carriers of institutional forces.

Routines as Carriers

Institutions may also be embodied in—carried by—structured activities in the form of habitualized behavior and routines. Routines
are carriers that rely on patterned actions that reflect the tacit knowledge of actors—deeply ingrained habits and procedures based on
inarticulated knowledge and beliefs.

Rather than privileging cultural systems, many early institutionalists viewed habitualized action, routines, standard operating procedures,
and similar patterned activities as the more central features of institutions. March and Simon (1958) pointed out that repetitive "performance
programs" were a central ingredient accounting for the reliability of
organizations. And more recently, evolutionary theorists, such as Nelson
and Winter (1982), point to the stabilizing role played by participants'
skills and organizational routines: activities involving little or no con-

scious choice and behavior governed by tacit knowledge and constrained by rules of which the actor may be unaware. Viewing routines as the "genes" of organizations, Winter (1990) points out that they range from "hard," that is, activities encoded into technologies, to "soft," that is, organizational routines such as assembly lines or fast-food procedures, but all involve "repetitive patterns of activity" (pp. 274-275).[5] Such routines underlie much of the stability of organizational behavior—accounting for their reliable performance as well as for their rigidities.

These arguments and distinctions suggest that organizations are deeply embedded in institutional contexts. A given organization is supported and constrained by institutional forces. Also, a given organization may incorporate institutional elements, in the form of cultures, structures, or routines, into its own system. It is appropriate to speak of the extent to which organizational elements are institutionalized. These views are shared by all, or the great majority of, institutional theorists. That subset endorsing a cognitive perspective would add an additional, even more fateful, assertion: The very concept of an organization as a special purpose, instrumental entity is itself a product of institutional processes—constitutive processes that define the capacities of collective actors. This version of institutional theory, in particular, tends to subvert or undermine the conventional distinction between organization and environment. Organizations are penetrated by environments in ways not encompassed by earlier theoretical models.

Varying Levels of Analysis

One of the principal ways in which the several varieties of institutional theory differ is in the level at which they are applied. Levels identified vary greatly in terms of whether the investigator is focusing on more micro or more macro phenomena. The key underlying dimension is the scope of the phenomena encompassed, whether measured in terms of space, time, or numbers of persons affected. For institutions, level may be usefully operationalized as the range of jurisdiction of the institutional form. Given the complexity and variety of social phenomena, any particular set of distinctions will be somewhat arbitrary. Nevertheless, for our purposes it is useful to identify six categories: the

levels of *world system, societal, organizational field, organizational population, organization,* and *organizational subsystem.*[6]

Most of these six levels are widely employed and recognizable to
social analysts; all are of interest to students of organizations. Perhaps
the least familiar, yet the level of most significance to institutional
theory, is that of the organizational field. Following DiMaggio and
Powell (1983), an organizational *field* refers to "those organizations
that, in the aggregate, constitute a recognized area of institutional life:
key suppliers, resource and product consumers, regulatory agencies,
and other organizations that produce similar services or products"
(p. 143). Hirsch (1985) has proposed the closely related concept of
"industry system," and Meyer and I have proposed that of "societal
sector" (Scott and Meyer 1983/1991). All of these conceptions build
on the more conventional concept of "industry"—a population of
organizations operating in the same domain as indicated by the similarity of their services of products—but adds to this focal population
those other and different organizations that critically influence their
performance. Fields are defined in terms of shared cognitive or normative frameworks or a common regulative system.

> The notion of field connotes the existence of a community of organizations
> that partakes of a common meaning system and whose participants interact
> more frequently and fatefully with one another than with actors outside of
> the field. (Scott 1994a, pp. 207-208)

An example of an organizational field would be an educational system
composed of a set of schools (focal population) and related organizations such as district offices and parent-teacher associations. Given the
definition of field, it is apparent that this conception provides a level
at which institutional forces are likely to be particularly salient.[7]

The other level of analysis somewhat distinctive to organizational
research and often employed in institutional studies is that of the population. *Populations* are defined as a collection or aggregate of organizations that are "alike in some respect," in particular to "classes of organizations that are relatively homogeneous in terms of environmental
vulnerability" (Hannan and Freeman 1977, p. 166). Newspaper companies or trade unions are examples of organizational populations.

Table 3.3   Institutional Pillars and Varying Levels: Illustrative Theorists

	Pillar		
Level	*Regulative*	*Normative*	*Cognitive*
World system	North and Thomas 1973	Krasner 1983	Meyer 1994
Societal	Skocpol 1979	Parsons 1953, 1960a	Dobbin 1994
Organizational field	Campbell and Lindberg 1990, Schmitter 1990	Mezias 1990	DiMaggio 1991
Organizational population	Barnett and Carroll 1993a	Singh, Tucker, and House 1986	Carroll and Hannan 1989
Organization	Williamson 1975, 1985, 1991	Selznick 1949	Clark 1970
Organizational subsystem	Shepsle and Weingast 1987	Roy 1952, Buroway 1979	Zimmerman 1969

Nevertheless, to reiterate, all six levels are of interest. And as with the notion of carriers, the levels distinction is orthogonal to and can be cross-classified with the set of institutional elements (see Table 3.3).

The entries in Table 3.3 refer to theorists whose work has pursued one or another institutional element at each of the specified levels. (Most of these studies are reviewed in more detail in subsequent chapters.) Briefly, Meyer (1994) examines institutional systems as cognitive forms operating at the level of the world system. Dobbin (1994) has examined the varying cultural belief systems that underlie societal policies affecting railway systems in the United States, England, and France. Working at the level of the organizational field, DiMaggio (1991) has studied the cultural belief systems constructed to support artistic organizations such as museums in the United States. Carroll and Hannan (1989) employ data on the density or prevalence of newspapers, viewed as an organizational population, as an indicator of the taken-for-grantedness of this organizational form. At the organization level, Clark (1970) has examined the distinctive cultural values cultivated by a set of elite colleges. And Zimmerman (1969), working at the subsystem level, has described the development of typifications and routines among intake work in a social welfare agency.

Turning to theorists emphasizing normative elements, Krasner (1983) and colleagues have examined the circumstances surrounding the development of common normative frameworks or "regimes" at the international level. Parsons (1953) has described differences in value systems and normative frameworks at the societal level and their consequences for organizations. Mezias (1990) has studied changes in normative beliefs regarding financial reporting requirements for corporations occasioned by the actions of state agents and professional accounting societies. Singh, Tucker, and House (1986) have examined the effects on survival rates in a population of voluntary social service organizations of being certified by public agencies. Selznick (1949) examined the ways in which procedural requirements became "infused with value" in the TVA. And Roy (1952) and Burawoy (1979) examined the institutionalization of normative frameworks regarding production and restriction of output among workers in a machine shop of a manufacturing plant.

Finally, among those theorists stressing the regulative aspects of institutions, North and Thomas (1973) have examined how the institution of property rights and associated state regulatory apparatus developed in the Western world during the 15th through the 17th centuries. Skocpol (1979) examined differences in the organization and operation of the state as it affected the course of revolutions occurring in France, Russia, and China. Analysts such as Schmitter (1990) and Campbell and Lindberg (1990) have examined the varying governance mechanisms at work in different societal sectors or industries. Barnett and Carroll (1993a) have studied the effects on the development of early telephone companies of various regulatory policies pursued by state and federal authorities. Williamson (1975, 1985, 1991) has developed his markets and hierarchies framework to explain the emergence of varying types of organizational forms to govern, and reduce the costs of, economic transactions. And Shepsle and Weingast (1987) have studied the institutional foundations of committee power in Congress.

More generally, as illustrated in Figure 3.1, it is possible to associate various schools or types of work with different locations in the property space created by the cross-classification of emphasis and level. Most of the neo-institutional work conducted by sociologists in the recent period is guided by the combination of a cognitive emphasis and attention to the macrolevels: processes operating at a trans-organizational level. Moreover, this work stresses cultural carriers—widespread beliefs, professional norms—but also attends to the im-

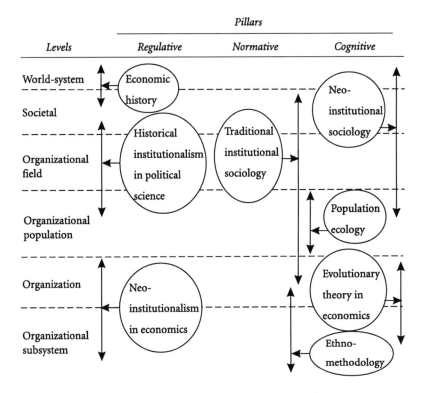

Figure 3.1. Institutional Pillars and Varying Levels: Illustrative Schools

pact of macro-structural carriers such as international organizations, the state, and trade and professional associations.

Attention to cognitive elements at the organization or organizational subsystem level has largely been provided by the ethnomethodologists and by students of corporate culture. The ethnomethodologists, along with some evolutionary economists, focus on habits and skills and so attend more closely to activities as carriers of institutions at the organizational and suborganizational levels (see Turner 1974).

The traditional institutional approach in sociology—work associated with Hughes, Parsons, and Selznick—is defined by a focus on normative elements and attention to levels ranging from the individual organization to the society. Both the cultural and structural carriers are emphasized in this approach.

Economists and political scientists are most likely to emphasize the regulative view of institutions. Economic historians focus on the macrolevels, examining the origins and functions of transnational and national rules and enforcement mechanisms that are developed to regulate economic behavior of firms and individuals. Historical institutionalists in both sociology and political science emphasize the study of regulatory regimes and governance mechanisms that operate at the societal and industry level. And the new institutionalists in economics along with the rational choice theorists in political science focus primarily on regulative processes operating at the organizational or suborganizational level. The economic historians and historical institutionalists emphasize cultural and structural carriers, whereas the new institutional economists emphasize primarily structural carriers.

We discover, then, substantial differences among current schools aligned with the new institutionalism. Sociologists pursuing this line of work emphasize a cognitive conception, cultural carriers, and macrolevel forces. By contrast, the new institutional economists stress a regulative conception, structural carriers, and a micro focus. Rather different perspectives to be sharing the same label!

Concluding Comment

Although it is possible to combine the insights of economic, political, and sociological analysts into a single, complex, integrated model of an institution, I believe it wiser at this point to recognize the differing assumptions and emphases that tend to accompany the models currently guiding inquiry into these phenomena. Three contrasting models of institutions are identified—the regulative, the normative, and the cognitive—although it is not possible to associate any of the disciplines uniquely with any of these proposed models. The models are differentiated such that each identifies a distinctive basis of compliance, mechanism of diffusion, type of logic, cluster of indicators, and foundation for legitimacy claims.

Two other distinctions are introduced in an attempt to recognize the flexibility and generality of institutions. First, institutions are viewed as varying in their mode of carrier or host. Institutions may be borne by cultures, social structures, or routines (and, perhaps, also by technologies). Second, institutions are described as capable of operating at—having jurisdiction over—differing levels; some are restricted to operating within organizational subunits, whereas others function at levels as broad as that of world systems. The variety of possible carriers through which institutions work, together with the multiple levels at which they operate, help to account both for why they receive so much attention and why they generate so much confusion and inconsistency among their observers.

Two sources of continuing controversy are also identified. First, institutions have become an important combat zone in the broader, ongoing disputation within the social sciences centering on the utility of rational choice theory for explaining human behavior. Are we to employ a more restricted, instrumental logic in accounting for the determinants and consequences of institutions or is it preferable to posit a broader, more socially embedded practical logic? Second, controversy exists as to whether to regard the world as existing independently of our socially constructed consciousness of it. There is no sign of quick or easy resolution to either of these debates because the battle is sustained by two of the enduring antinomies underlying our science.

Notes

1. This integrated model of institutions is elaborated in Scott (1994c).

2. Another candidate for an institutional pillar is cathectic or emotional elements. Parsons (1951), in particular, emphasized the importance of emotion-laden attachments to practices or relations that provide not only a motivational basis but a kind of logic of action: behavior guided by the "habits of the heart." D'Andrade (1984) also stresses that meaning systems have an evocative as well as a cognitive aspect. They evoke not only ideas but feelings and desires, and the latter no less than the former are part of the cultural meaning of symbols.

3. In a related formulation, Bourdieu (1990) argues the necessity of focusing on relations and processes rather than on actors and structures.

4. In this distinction, authority is viewed as "legitimate" power or as "normatively regulated" power (see Dornbusch and Scott 1975; Scott 1992, p. 307).

5. A fourth candidate as a carrier of institutions is *technology,* defined narrowly as material artifacts within which are embedded knowledge and skills (see Barley 1986; Orlikowski 1992). Like other modalities of action-structure, technology is, on the one hand, socially constructed by the actions of designers, technologists, investors, and others. On the other hand, once developed, it tends "to become reified and institutionalized, losing its connection with the human agents that constructed it or gave it meaning [and so appears] to be part of the objective, structural properties of the organization" (Orlikowski 1992, p. 406).

6. For a related discussion of institutional theories that highlights differences in levels of analysis, see Scott (1994b).

7. Bourdieu (1988) has developed a general conception of social "field" not restricted to organizations. In Bourdieu's conception, all societies contain an assemblage of fields governed by distinctive values and logics. Fields are in part structured by habitus: dispositional orientations shared by agents within the field. Bourdieu views a field as "a relational configuration" containing a patterned system of forces. "A field is simultaneously a space of conflict and competition" in which "participants vie to establish monopoly over the species of capital effective in it" (Bourdieu and Wacquant 1992, p. 17).

4 Explaining Institutions

Empirical Research

The concerted efforts to revive interest in institutional analysis and to connect these arguments to organizations began in the mid-1970s. It is not surprising that most of the early statements were primarily theoretical, employing evidence in only a casual and illustrative manner. However, it was not long before various types of empirical investigations began to appear. Their numbers have steadily increased, so that by now, a substantial amount of research relevant to the testing of institutional arguments has been produced. Most of this work treats institutional frameworks as given and asks how they affect organizational structures and functions. That is, in most of the empirical literature, institutions are treated as independent variables and the studies are directed to examining their effects on organizations, organizational populations, or organizational fields. This focus is understandable because students of organizations are primarily interested in assessing whether and to what extent institutional systems affect individual organizations or collections of organizations. If such influences cannot be demonstrated, there would be little incentive for these analysts to pursue the related questions regarding the sources of institutions.

Chapters 5 and 6 review and discuss the larger literature on institutional effects. The current chapter considers the question of institutional determinants.

It is helpful to divide the question of institutional determinants into two parts: (1) how are institutions developed or changed? and (2) how are institutions maintained and diffused? Before addressing these questions, however, I call attention to a distinction that cuts across the full range of studies of institutions, affecting what questions are asked and what methods are employed. This is the "process versus variance" distinction. Although not restricted to institutional analysis, this distinction is especially evident in current efforts to explain the development of institutions.

Variance and Process
Approaches to Explaining Institutions

In an important early article on the subject, Zucker (1977) observed that "institutionalization is both a process and a property variable" (p. 728). That is, for some purposes, we treat an institution as an entity, as a cultural or social system, characterized by one or more features or properties. On other occasions, we are interested in institutionalization as a process, as the development over time of regulative, normative, or cognitive systems capable, to varying degrees, of providing meaning and stability to social behavior. Although the two views obviously are closely related, our modes of analysis tend to emphasize one or the other, and the theoretical frameworks and methodologies we employ also are likely to vary, as Mohr (1982) has emphasized (see also Scott 1994b).

Mohr (1982) differentiates between variance and process theories. *Variance theories*, associated with viewing institutions as entities, focus attention on abstract variables, independent and dependent, and attempt to establish their causal relations. Precursor (independent) variables are seen as a necessary and sufficient condition for determining the values of outcome (dependent) variables. Although precursor variables predate outcome variables, the time ordering among the precursor variables themselves is viewed as immaterial to the outcome. Variance theories address the question: *Why* did the observed effect happen?

They attempt to identify what factors were associated with the observed characteristics of the phenomena of interest.

By contrast, *process theories* deal with "a series of occurrences of events rather than a set of relations among variables" (Mohr 1982, p. 54). In process theories, time is of the essence, in particular, the time ordering of the contributory events. "In a process analysis, events are represented as taking place sequentially in real time" (Langlois 1986a, p. 7). A process approach addresses the question: *How* did the observed effects happen? This approach assumes that "history matters," that how things occur influences what things happen (Scott 1983).

History always matters in the sense that "effects follow causes in temporal succession," but David (1988) argues that some historical processes matter more than others. Thus some outcomes appear to require long sequences of events—for example, the buildup of industrial structures or the creation of human capital. Other events arise through a branching process such that once a particular choice occurs, other possibilities are foreclosed. Such outcomes are regarded as "path dependent" and are of particular interest to social scientists because they can result in "locked-in" structures that may be demonstrably inferior (less efficient) than alternative options. A variety of self-reinforcing feedback mechanisms supporting "path dependent processes make it difficult for organizations to explore alternative options" (Powell 1991, p. 193).

Process theories in economics can also be contrasted to the static conception of equilibrium that undergirds neoclassical theory. Mainstream economic analysts posit an equilibrium condition without attempting to theorize how stable economic conditions—including the institutional arrangements that undergird them—come into existence, as well as how these arrangements undergo change (see Hodgson 1988; Nelson 1986).

Process theories vary in their degree of formalization. Most often, a process argument is little more than a historical account—a narrative frequently consisting of "stage-naming" concepts that provide a description of a sequence of events. Economists refer to such explanations, rather pejoratively, as "storytelling" (Knudsen 1993).

Explanations of particular institutions can easily become "historicist," favoring "interpretations that stress the complexity, uniqueness, and contingency of historical events" (Kiser and Hechter 1991, p. 10). The most popular approach in contemporary historical sociology involves "inductive generalism": the examination of one or more cases employed to generate and assess historically limited explanations (Kiser and Hechter 1991). Here there are attempts to develop or to apply general theories but recognition that the generalizations are relative—and may be limited—to a certain context or set of conditions (Skocpol 1984, p. 376).

More rigorous and highly formalized approaches attempt to specify explicitly the nature of the probabilistic process that connects events with outcomes (see Lave and March (1975). Game theorists such as Schotter (1986) and Sugden (1986) have developed mathematical models of the processes by which rule systems or sets of conventions evolve from repeated game situations played by rational actors; the models are typically assessed through experiments or computer simulations. And economic historians, such as Arthur (1988) and David (1988), have employed Markov models to depict path-dependent processes related to institution building and institutional change.

Creating and Changing Institutions

One of the prevailing criticisms of contemporary institutional theory is that it pays insufficient attention to change in institutional systems (e.g., see DiMaggio 1988, p. 12; Brint and Karabel 1991, p. 343). Although this criticism may once have been on the mark, there now exist a substantial number of studies of this important topic addressing the full range of institutional elements. As discussed in Chapter 3, institutional theorists differ in the primacy they ascribe to the various elements that form institutions. Depending on whether they privilege regulative, normative, or cognitive elements, analysts provide somewhat different accounts of the development of institutions or changes in existing institutions. Consider the following process-oriented studies.

Process Approaches

Regulative Elements

Theorists emphasizing a regulative view of institutions are likely to embrace a rational choice framework. In considering why institutions exist, the critical question confronted by rational choice theorists is to determine when—under what conditions—it is in an actor's self-interest to construct and maintain institutional structures that will govern not only others' but one's own behavior.

I examine two studies emphasizing regulative aspects of institutions employing a process approach. One of the most wide-ranging and well-known studies of this type at the world system level is the historical account provided by North and Thomas (1973) of the "rise of the Western world." These economic historians argue that economic growth will not occur unless there are mechanisms to closely align social and private rates of return. Individuals will be motivated to undertake socially desirable activities only if they provide private benefits that exceed private costs. This situation in turn requires that property rights be established and enforced. The need for such regulative institutions, however, does not guarantee their development. Creating such structures is costly. Although governments take over the enforcement of property rights because they can do so at lower costs than can private volunteer groups, their fiscal needs may encourage them to enforce agreements that do not promote economic growth. Hence "we have no guarantee that productive institutional arrangements will emerge" (North and Thomas 1973, p. 8).

North and Thomas review historical evidence from the High Middle Ages to the beginning of the 16th century, noting developments in the political economy of Europe that advanced or depressed economic growth. They conclude that by the beginning of the 18th century, "a structure of property rights had developed in the Netherlands and England which provided the incentives necessary for sustained economic growth" (North and Thomas 1973). Although their particular interpretation of history has not gone unchallenged (see, e.g., Wallerstein 1979), North and Thomas do provide a careful examination of concrete historical situations as they seek to discover which groups promoted and benefited from the development of various types of enforcement institutions.

Sociologists working from a rational choice framework (who typically emphasize a bounded rationality rather than a stronger version of rationality) have tended to focus their attention not on the development of more efficient forms but rather on the emergence of rules and governance structures that will support the development of a stable order, protecting the interests of all by curbing the asocial behavior of each. Thus Coleman (1990) argues that externalities of others' actions affecting our own interests creates a demand for controlling rules or norms, but whether a regulative structure will in fact develop depends on the nature of the social relationships among those whose interests are affected. Similarly, Hechter (1990) argues that the creation of the stronger form of cooperative institution requires some basis for the development of solidarity, imposed or voluntary, among those who both stand to gain but also will be subject to the new institutional controls.

An interesting example of this process, focusing on the development of regulative institutions at the level of the organizational field, is provided by Stern's (1979) study of the evolution of the National Collegiate Athletic Association (NCAA) in the United States during the first half of this century. He describes how a small, loose confederation designed for mutual support at the time of its founding was forged into "a powerful control agent capable of inflicting serious financial loss on member schools caught violating its rules" (p. 247). Stern combines a network approach that examines changes in administrative structures, system coupling, multiplexity of ties, and the emergence of new network resources with a process view that examines "the activities through which change takes place" (p. 246). Stern's analysis shows that although over time the central administration structure grew in size and controlled more resources, this potential power did not become the basis for a genuine enforcement system until highly publicized scandals together with the threat of outside intervention induced the council to adopt an "enforcement decision," requiring participation by all conference schools and backing its provisions with sanctions.

Normative Elements

Three examples of process studies of the normative elements of institutions reflect work at the organization, organizational field, and individual actor levels: Selznick's (1949) influential study of the TVA, the study by Leblebici and colleagues (Leblebici, Salancik, Copay, and King 1991) of institutional change in the U.S. radio industry, and Axelrod's (1984) imaginative study of cooperation.

Selznick (1949) provides a basically historical account of the development over time of a distinctive ideology and set of normative commitments on the part of TVA officials. As I noted in reviewing Selznick's views in Chapter 2, his approach describes how the original structure and goals of this government agency were transformed over time by the commitments of its participants to the means of action—to particular ways of conducting work and, more important, to the survival of the organization itself. The latter commitment had the unintended consequence of allowing powerful external constituents, in return for their support, to influence and compromise organizational goals. In Selznick's (1957) work, to institutionalize is "to infuse with value" (p. 17) as intrinsic worth is accorded to a structure or process that originally possessed only instrumental value. Selznick emphasizes normative beliefs and interpersonal commitments rather than cognitive frames or scripts.

Selznick's approach focuses on internal relations, especially informal structures rather than on formal structures, and on the immediate environment of organizations rather than on more general cultural rules or characteristics of wider organizational fields (see DiMaggio and Powell 1991, pp. 11-15). The carriers of institutionalized values are organizational structures, in particular, informal structures and co-optative relations linking the organization with salient external actors, both individual and collective.

The importance of social power is emphasized—the vesting of interests in informal structures and the co-optation of external groups who acquire internal power in return for their support. Selznick's analysis of the TVA examines the ways in which particular constituencies, such as the agricultural interests, on whom the organization was dependent, were able to modify agency programs in ways that compromised its conservation program. And, as discussed in Chapter 2, Stinchcombe's (1968) amplification of Selznick's arguments stresses the ways in which power can be used to perpetuate these interests or values over time.[1]

In their study of institutional practices in the U.S. radio broadcasting industry, Leblebici and colleagues (Leblebici et al. 1991) describe changes occurring during the period 1920-1965, identifying three stages of development. The stages are defined in terms of who the dominant players were, what served as the medium of exchange, and what institutionalized practices governed these exchanges. The problem posed by these investigators is: "Why do those who occupy the positions of power in the existing institutions willingly change its practices?" (Leblebici et al. 1991, p. 337). Their analysis suggests that, at least in this industry and during the period under study, change was primarily endogenous, involving innovations introduced by marginal participants in the market that were later adopted by leading members driven to do so by intense competition. These new practices became conventions when used recurrently, and subsequently became "institutional practices by acquiring a normative character, when sustained through some form of legitimacy" (p. 342).

This study provides a clear description of changes in this organizational field over time: changes in the types and numbers of players, in the changing bases of competition and "medium of transactions," and in the nature of the coordination or governance problems posed. Dominant organizations are viewed as imposing order on the field and as making changes in this order only when forced to do so by competitors who threaten their position. Whereas diffusion of practices throughout the field is described, the emergence of supporting norms is inferred rather than documented.

Axelrod (1984) has employed the prisoner's dilemma situation to examine the conditions under which individuals who pursue their own self-interest in the absence of a central authority will evolve norms of cooperation. The prisoner's dilemma constructs a situation in which two players make one of two choices: cooperation (c) or noncooperation (n). The payoff matrix is such that if both players opt for c then both receive an intermediate reward; if both select n they receive a low reward; but if one player selects c when the other selects n, the former (sucker) receives no reward while the latter (exploiter) receives a high reward. Players are not allowed to exchange any type of information other than their choices, and the game is played over a number of trials.

In a novel design, Axelrod invited other game theorists from many disciplines to compete in a computer tournament to select the best game strategy by submitting a program that embodies rules to select the cooperative or noncooperative choice on each move. Such a program provides a complete process description of the sequence of decisions during the course of the encounter. Of the 14 strategies submitted, the most successful was the "TIT-FOR-TAT" decision rule: a strategy that starts with a cooperative choice and thereafter does whatever the other player did on the previous move. This simple strategy provided the best payoff to the player adopting it under a wide range of simulated conditions. Axelrod (1984) summarizes its virtues:

What accounts for TIT-FOR-TAT's robust success is its combination of being nice, retaliatory, forgiving, and clear. Its niceness [never initiating noncooperation] prevents it from getting into unnecessary trouble. Its retaliation discourages the other side from persisting whenever defection is tried. Its forgiveness helps restore mutual cooperation. And its clarity makes it intelligible to the other player, thereby eliciting long-term cooperation. (p. 54)

Although it may be argued that the prisoner's dilemma is just a game, it encapsulates an important dilemma built into many real-world situations, from the school yard to international diplomacy. It is to cope with such situations that security regimes and similar types of institutions develop (see Krasner 1983; Mares and Powell 1990). A particularly important element of the conditions supporting the rise of stable cooperative norms is that "the future must have a sufficiently large shadow" (Axelrod 1984, p. 174). The anticipation of future interaction provides an important stimulus to evoke norms of reciprocity; indeed, such norms are argued to undergird the stability of much ongoing economic and social behavior, rendering less necessary the expensive alternative to resort to external regulative structures such as the legal system (see Macaulay 1963).[2]

Cognitive Elements

A number of recent empirical studies employ a process approach to the examination of changes in the cognitive aspects of institutions. I examine three, each conducted at a different level of analysis. Working at the societal level, Hirsch (1986) studied changes in the symbolic framing of hostile corporate takeovers occurring in the United States between 1965 and 1986. DiMaggio's (1991) study of the efforts by professionals to create the cultural conditions that would support the development and maintenance of art museums during the late 19th century in America is cast at the organizational field level. And Barley's (1986) study of the changes in the social order of radiological departments within hospitals occasioned by the introduction of new technology is conducted at the organizational subsystem level.

All three studies focus on cognitive features: Hirsch on changes in discourse or the language employed to characterize hostile takeovers, DiMaggio on the creation of cultural distinctions between high and low forms of art and the creation and selection of cultural models for constituting art museums as distinctive types of organizations, and Barley on changes in the scripts employed to guide activities and interactions between radiologists and technologists. Barley employs quantitative techniques to evaluate changes in scripts over time, and Hirsch provides a relatively systematic description of changes in images and frames used to depict takeovers across three time periods. DiMaggio's approach is less systematic but includes detailed discussion of alternative constitutive models for museums, including one that succeeded and one that failed. Barley and Hirsch emphasize the interdependence between ongoing activities and interpretations of actions. Institutional structures are seen as both product and context: Cultural rules are changed by ongoing activities but at the same time act as constraints and guides to future activities. This process-oriented "structuration" model (see Giddens 1984) of social order is made particularly explicit in both Barley's and DiMaggio's accounts.

Each of these studies tells us what happened, described as changes in activities and meanings occurring in real time. Both Hirsch and Barley identify explicit stages in describing the changes that occurred. Hirsch, however, does not attempt to indicate how the changes occurred, by what actions or mechanisms the observed changes in language were brought about. By contrast, DiMaggio (1988) argues that the question of institutional origins provides an opportunity to bring agency (actors intentionally pursuing interests) back into institutional analysis. He asserts: "New institutions arise when organized actors with sufficient resources (*institutional entrepreneurs*) see in them an opportunity to realize interests that they value highly" (DiMaggio 1988, p. 14). DiMaggio borrows heavily on Bourdieu's conception of social fields as structured by competition and conflict among competing players (see Bourdieu and Wacquant 1992).

Both Barley and DiMaggio give clear accounts of who these actors were and what actions they took to bring about the changes. In Barley's account, the resulting changes in the social order—changed meanings, roles, and decision-making structure—appear to have been unselfconscious and unanticipated. A technological innovation occurred and, in responding to it, similar types of actors in two different hospital settings reacted in ways that were somewhat similar but also somewhat distinctive: The two social structures were altered in ways determined by the processes that produced them. For DiMaggio, the principal actors—the Carnegie Corporation, the academic art historians, and the elite patrons—were more self-conscious agents, pursuing together a "professional project" that would advance and protect their own interests. However, in addition to developing and installing a distinctive organizational form, their actions also resulted—as an unintended consequence—in the increased structuration of the organizational field. Finally, more so than the other analysts, DiMaggio attempts to develop generalizations—inductive hypotheses—about factors affecting such developments.[3]

Variance Approaches

As noted, variance approaches attend more to identifying the factors causally associated with the phenomena of interest. I illustrate this approach for each of the three conceptions of institutions.

Regulative Elements

Williamson (1975, 1985) is the primary contemporary proponent of viewing institutional arrangements in organizations as regulative systems: as governance structures. As discussed in Chapter 3, he has developed an explanatory framework within which economic agents are expected to devise or select those governance forms that will minimize transaction costs. Two empirical studies testing Williamson's arguments will be briefly described.

Walker and Weber (1984) tested Williamson's (1981) arguments that transactions involving higher uncertainty and greater asset specificity (specialized skills or machinery) would be more likely to be produced rather than purchased by the firm—that is, governed by the firm's hierarchy rather than governed by the market. Their study of 60 "make or buy" decisions within a division of a large automobile company found results generally consistent with these predictions although, unexpectedly, the researchers found that comparative production costs had a larger impact on these decisions than did transaction costs. Note that in this study the question is not which governance system the company is to create but rather, for a given type of decision, which of two existing alternative governance systems to use: the organizations hierarchy or the market.

Studies by Armour and Teece (1978) and by Teece (1981) attempt to evaluate empirically Williamson's arguments regarding the relation

between a firm's governance structure and its economic performance. Following Chandler's (1962) early insights and historical research, Williamson (1975) argued that firms adopting a multidivisional
(M-form) structure would be more capable of separating strategic
from operational decision making, allocating capital, and monitoring divisional performance. Armour and Teece studied a sample of
diversified firms in the petroleum industry and found that those firms
adopting the M-form structure performed better financially. Teece
extended the test to evaluate the performance of pairs of firms matched
in size and product line in 20 industries. The performance of the firm
first adopting the M-form (the "lead" firm) was compared with that
of the matched firm for two time periods.

> If the lead firm in the "before" period was the superior performer, support
> for the M-form hypothesis would require the differential to narrow in the
> "after" period; conversely, if the lead firm was not the superior performer
> in the "before" period, support for the M-form hypothesis would require
> the differential to widen in the "after" period. (Teece 1981, p. 180)

The data supported the hypothesis.

Williamson, in concert with other practitioners of the new institutional economics, argues in effect that managers will attempt to design
the boundaries and the governance structures of their firms so as to
economize on transaction costs. This emphasis, as David (1992) observes, assumes that these institutional arrangements represent "pres-
ently efficient solutions to resource allocation problems and that
institutional arrangements are perfectly malleable" (pp. 2-3). Such
assumptions are at odds with those held by most sociologists and
economic historians who stress the effect of past events on present
institutions and the capacity of these structures to resist change. But
even though the new institutional economists argue as if institutions
can be readily changed, they also tend to employ functionalist
arguments (see Granovetter 1985; Yarbrough and Yarbrough 1990)—
a type of explanation that is likely to be used when the phenomenon
to be explained has persistent features that involve "homeostatic"
variables (see Knudsen 1993), an important feature of institutions to
be discussed in the following section.

Functional explanations attempt to account for the existence and
maintenance of a given social structure (institution) by noting what

functions it performs for participants' adaptation: The consequences of an arrangement are used to explain its existence and persistence. To be a valid functional argument, when a given behavior or structure is claimed to be responsible for producing a desired homeostatic effect, the analyst must specify the causal feedback loop by which the forces maintaining the structure are selected or reinforced (see Stinchcombe 1968, pp. 87-93). Few functional explanations meet this criterion. Most analysts are content to argue "as if" rather than to "demonstrate that" such forces are at work (Elster 1983). And, as Fligstein (1990) observes, most analysts find that it is easier to read history backward:

> The central mistake made in traditional accounts of the history of the large corporation is that by reading history backwards economic historians have known how things turned out and thereby were able to impute what kind of social institutions must have been called forth by efficient markets. (p. 300)

Normative Elements

An example of a variance approach to accounting for the creation of an institution composed of normative rules is provided by Leblebici and Salancik's (1982) study of rule making conducted by the Chicago Board of Trade. Although they begin by providing a process account of the evolution of the board from a small private club in the 1850s to its current form, they shift to a variance model in explaining how uncertainty in prices is associated with the formulation of rules and sanctions. Market volatility with respect to specific commodities was found to correlate positively with the emergence of secondary rules—rules that coordinate exchanges and allow them to take place—whereas total volume of transactions, measuring the general health of the market, was found to be negatively associated with primary rules—rules dealing with issues of governance and rules that determine what kinds of market transactions can take place. Leblebici and Salancik (1982) employ a functionalist explanation of these relations:

> It is argued that the very uncertainty of the exchange process itself forces upon exchange members a need to develop an interorganizational organization. This organization, like other organizations, creates working rules to regulate its members and an authority system to enforce them. These rules enable exchanges to occur within the interorganizational field with a predictability and stability they otherwise would not have. (p. 228)

These authors, however, fail to specify the causal feedback loop by which these rules are reproduced.

Cognitive Elements

Viewing institutions as constitutive rules for structuring organizations, Suchman (1994, forthcoming) examined factors affecting the institutionalization of venture capital financing practices in California's Silicon Valley during the period 1975-1990. Suchman analyzed data on 108 venture capital financing contracts from two Silicon Valley venture capital funds. Such contracts bring together the venture capitalists, lawyers, and entrepreneurs in the crucial founding event, constituting the structure of relations between these parties as they jointly form the start-up company. The contracts were coded along numerous dimensions, and these scores were then used to calculate measures of contractual standardization as an indicator of increasing institutionalization. Suchman's analysis reveals that standardization was strongly correlated to both date of filing and location of the law firm that drafted the contract. In general, standardization of contracts was greater the later in the time period they were filed and the closer the location of the law firm drafting the contract was to the core of Silicon Valley.

Another study examining factors affecting the cognitive aspects of institutions considers changes occurring over a much longer period—1870 to the present—and focuses on the societal level of analysis. Barley and Kunda (1992) use historical information to document changes in managerial ideology in the United States. Their analysis reveals the existence of "five distinct rhetorics that have left their mark on American managerial thought and practice" (p. 364), the discourse shifting back and forth between periods emphasizing more normative and more rational control strategies. They then attempt to relate these shifts in dominant rhetoric to the pattern of economic expansion and contraction. Their analysis indicates that rational rhetoric was likely to be associated with economic upswings during which there were higher returns to capital, whereas normative discourse was associated with downswings when the economy contracted. They reason that managers will be "attracted to rhetorics that emphasize rational procedures and structures when profits hinge easily on capital investment and automation" but turn to normative rhetorics, emphasizing the motivation of labor, when returns on capital begin to decline (p. 391).

Barley and Kunda argue that their analysis is an attempt to combine idealist and materialist explanations of ideological change, materialist factors helping to account for the timing of trends, and idealist factors accounting for the cultural constraints within time periods. Although no data are presented to support the argument, the authors attempt to more explicitly introduce agency into their discussion by suggesting that "each surge of managerial theorizing was championed by members of a specific subgroup whose interests were thereby advanced" (Barley and Kunda 1992, p. 393).

Rational Versus Practical Action

The selection of empirical studies of institution building by no means is a random or representative sample of the literature. Nevertheless, it may be useful to determine the types of arguments represented with respect to whether rational or broader practical explanations are provided. It appears that five of the studies rely primarily on rational arguments: the deliberate selection of institutional arrangements that served the decision maker's primary interests. Each of the studies by DiMaggio, Leblebici and Salancik, Axelrod, Armour and Teece, and Walker and Weber provides an account in which individuals design institutions that serve their interests. Note, however, that the interests pursued by DiMaggio's actors are, in effect, social power; the other studies, primarily by economists, focus on monetary returns.

Several studies portray the operation of a more practical logic. Leblebici and Salancik's discussion of rule making by the Board of Trade and Suchman's account of increased standardization of contracts in Silicon Valley imply that actors are creating structures to minimize uncertainty—to construct stable and meaningful social arrangements. Barley and Kunda's account of the alternation of more normative and rational control strategies and Hirsch's analysis of the reframing of corporate takeovers also seem to be driven more by the actors' attempts at sensemaking—constructing plausible action rationales—than by narrow instrumental concerns.

In several of the studies, conflicting interests are at stake and some actors are more advantaged by the resulting institutional structures than are others, but the analysis suggests that the resulting institutional arrangements were more governed by unintended consequences than by conscious design. This appears to be the case in Selznick's account of the TVA, Barley's study of the radiological departments, and North and Thomas's historical discussion of property rights systems in early Europe. Stern too stresses inadvertence. He describes the creation of a governance structure with increased capacity to regulate member actions, but one that goes unused until external events intervene, requiring action.

Maintaining and Diffusing Institutions

As discussed in Chapter 3, the concept of institution connotes stability and persistence. However, as I have suggested, the basis for this quality—what mechanisms underlie stability—is in dispute. In particular, the underlying conception of institution—whether cognitive, normative, or regulative—affects views of maintenance mechanisms. Cognitive theorists tend to emphasize the important role played by unconscious, taken-for-granted assumptions defining social reality. As Zucker (1977) argues: "Internalization, self-reward, or other intervening processes need not be present to ensure cultural persistence because social knowledge once institutionalized exists as a fact, as part of objective reality, and can be transmitted directly on that basis" (p. 726).

Of course, social knowledge systems are themselves the subjects of power contests. It is by attaining control over these systems that professionals have attained and exercise their powers in modern society (see Chapter 5). Although power processes are sometimes underemphasized by cognitive theorists, regulative theorists are more likely to stress the importance of interest, agency, and social power: Actors employ power to protect their valued interests, and they use power to see that these interests are secure over time (see Stinchcombe 1968; DiMaggio 1988). Powell (1991) suggests, however, that in those cases involving weaker regulative institutional forms, such as conventions, power may play a reduced role in explaining persistence. He notes: "Persistence may not depend upon active agency because a particular practice or structure is so embedded in a network of practices and procedures that change in any one aspect requires changes in many other elements" (Powell 1991, p. 191). For example, many industry-wide product standards, exhibiting both influence and persistence, seem to be of this character (see Hemenway 1975).

Theorists taking a normative view emphasize the stabilizing influence of shared norms that are both internalized and imposed by others as well as the beneficial effects of legitimation on persistence. Kilduff (1993), for example, emphasizes the role of social networks whose members draw "on shared normative frameworks, continually monitor[ing] interpersonal behavior" and of accounts as part of the "reflexive monitoring" that maintains "an interpretive and normative base" to support ongoing behavior in a multinational corporation (pp. 265-266).

Perhaps, however, the power perspective and the more normative/cognitive view are not necessarily incompatible. DiMaggio (1991) and Brint and Karabel (1991) suggest that power is most apparent in the activities of those who construct the organizational field: those who create the categories, the norms, the rules and standards. Once such arrangements are in place, then local actors are likely to take them as given, as legitimate, and as authoritative. Their complacency helps to stabilize existing patterns.

Yet the amount of passivity and complacency involved in maintaining institutions should not be overstated. Whereas the ecological view that labels stability as "inertia" connotes a relatively inactive posture, newer institutional views emphasize the extent to which the persistence of cultures, structures, and activities relies on active monitoring of the social-cultural environment and the importance of continuing connections to the world outside the organization (see Westney 1993).

Rather than assuming that organizational inertia is the normal state and hence regarding institutional stability as not requiring explanation, Zucker (1988b) suggests that entropy—"a tendency toward disorganization in the social system" (p. 26)—is a more common tendency in organizations. Zucker argues that deinstitutionalization is prevalent and has many roots: flawed social transmission, inadequate socialization, the intrusion of personal characteristics and interests, and changed circumstances that render current practices or beliefs outmoded or ineffectual. (For a general review of the political, functional, and social sources of deinstitutionalization, see Oliver 1992.) Such arguments suggest that stability or persistence of social behaviors require explanation.

Stinchcombe (1968) provides a helpful discussion of two broad types of explanations that attempt to address stability or continuity of behavior: functionalist explanations, discussed above, and historicist explanations. Stinchcombe defines a historicist explanation as "one in which an effect created by causes at some previous period becomes a cause of that same effect in succeeding periods" (p. 103). For example, investments made in a company at a given time may account for its productivity; these same investments may also account for its productivity at a later time because of "sunk costs": the continuing value of the capital equipment and skilled labor and the likelihood that these resources will remain in the same place.

Although functionalist explanations were at first regarded as an alternative to historicist explanations, they are more appropriately regarded as closely related. Stinchcombe argues that historicist explanations generally account for "which of a set of functional alternatives is found in a particular society," whereas functionalist arguments are employed to account for the survival of that alternative when confronted with other possibilities.

Process Approaches to Maintenance

There appear to be relatively few process studies that explicitly focus on the ways in which institutional structures are maintained. Even though stability is the essence of institutions, most process studies focus on institutional change. Theoretical discussions by sociological neo-institutionalists such as Berger and Luckmann emphasize the ways in which intersubjective cognitive structures are preserved through interaction and socialization. In their discussion of the multiple factors conducing toward organizational inertia—another term for stability—Hannan and Freeman (1984) give primacy to the normative and regulative constraints:

> Some of the factors that generate structural inertia are internal to organizations: these include sunk costs in plant, equipment, and personnel, the dynamics of political coalitions and the tendency for precedents to become normative standards. Others are external. There are legal and other barriers to entry and exit. . . . Exchange relations with other organizations constitute an investment . . . [and] attempting radical structural change often threatens legitimacy. (p. 149)

And Stinchcombe's (1968, pp. 108-117) discussion, which stresses a more regulative conception, emphasizes the ability of those in power to control selection, socialization, and the conditions of incumbency of their successors.

Four examples of process studies of maintenance will be briefly described. In the first, a study of a mission organization that has survived for almost two centuries, virtually all of the forces supporting persistence—regulative, normative, and cognitive—appear to be at work. A Pietist enterprise, the Basel Mission, was founded in the early 19th century to educate missionaries and establish evangelical out-posts in various parts of the world. Miller (1994) has examined the records of this organization, focusing on the period 1815-1915, to ascertain the basis for its longevity. He argues that participants were recruited from a relatively homogeneous social base; were given inten-sive socialization so that participants came to share similar beliefs and values; were placed in a strong authority structure combining aspects of charismatic, traditional, and bureaucratic control elements to-gether with formalized procedures of "mutual surveillance"; and were encouraged to develop a sense of "specialness and separation" that insulated them from the corruption of the secular world.

In their study of the evolution over a 35-year period of a new industry devoted to the cochlear implant—a device to restore hearing to the deaf—Van de Ven and Garud (1994) analyze a series of events coded as creating variation (novel technical events), selection (rule-making events), and retention (rule-following events). The latter events, retention, are indicators of institutional persistence because they refer to an event that "was programmed or governed by existing institutional rules and routines" (Van de Ven and Garud 1994, p. 429).[4] Viewed over the period of study, their data show how novel technical events dominated during the developmental period from 1956 to 1983, rule-making and rule-following events grew in an oscillatory fashion during the middle period from 1983 to 1986, and then by 1989, "no more institutional rule-making events occurred while rule-fol-lowing events continued to occur" (p. 430). They also describe how institutional rules operated to suppress innovation and to "constrain the flexibility of private firms to adapt to changing circumstances" as existing technologies were locked in to specific technological paths.

Two other studies examine the persistence of workplace cultures in spite of the introduction of significant technological changes. Burawoy

(1979) was able to return to a machine shop studied by Roy (1952) some 30 years earlier. Although Burawoy's primary emphasis is on the changes that had occurred in this setting, the overwhelming message is one of substantial continuity. Both Roy and Burawoy stress "how the organization of a piecework machine shop gives rise to making out and how this in turn becomes the basis of shop-floor culture" (Burawoy 1979, p. 65). Both provide detailed descriptions of the construction of shared-meaning systems among workers and between workers and managers that give rise to stable patterns of behavior—both cooperation and conflict—on the shop floor.

Murphree (1987) has reviewed a number of surveys and conducted her own case study to examine the persistence of institutionalized sexism: factors that have prevented female secretaries in office situations from improving their relative power and status even after the introduction of new information technologies. She finds that the most common structural change is that a secretary now works for several bosses rather than for one. This change, however, has not dislodged the "patrimonial" relation existing between most secretaries and their superiors, described in detail by Kanter (1977), such that the secretary's status and discretion are largely determined by the status, preferences, and whims of the secretary's superior(s).

As indicated, however, relatively few studies document the persistence of institutional forms. Even among those few that deal with the topic, attention is focused more on showing *that* the forms persist rather than examining *how* they are reproduced. Until quite recently, much of the literature dealing with institutional stability has been produced by Marxist and feminist analysts, two sets of scholars who are interested in attempting to document both the existence and the persistence of inequitable and oppressive structures. Of late, there has been growing interest among scholars in examining social factors influencing the development of technology or even the coevolution of organizational structures and technology, illustrated above in the study by Van de Ven and Garud. This work examines the effects of social factors, both those that stimulate the invention of new technologies or structural arrangements but also those that cause them to pursue certain paths rather than others and operate to lock in particular variants (see Bijker, Hughes, and Pinch 1987; Baum and Singh 1994).

Variance Approaches to Maintenance

Zucker (1977) provides an early and influential analysis of factors accounting for three facets of institutional persistence: uniformity, maintenance, and resistance to change of cultural beliefs across generations of actors. Although she refers to her research as focusing on institutionalization processes, her approach is better described as one emphasizing variance. Her experimental study used the classic Sherif stimuli, asking subjects to evaluate the amount of apparent movement of a stationary light in a darkened room. Extent of institutionalization was manipulated by instructions given to the subjects: To create lower institutionalization, the subject was told only that the other person (a confederate) was "another person"; to create intermediate levels of institutionalization, the subject was told that she and her co-worker (the confederate) were both "members of an organization" but their positions were unspecified; and to create higher levels of institutionalization, the subject was told that she and her co-worker were both participants in an organization and the co-worker (the confederate) was given the title of "light operator." Zucker (1977) reasoned:

> Settings can vary in the degree to which acts in them are institutionalized. By being embedded in broader contexts where acts are viewed as institutionalized, acts in specific situations come to be viewed as institutionalized. Indicating that a situation is structured like situations in an organization makes the actors assume that the actions required of them by other actors in that situation will be . . . more regularized and that the interaction will be more definitely patterned than if the situation were not embedded in an organizational context.
>
> Any act performed by the occupant of an office is seen as highly objectified and exterior. When an actor occupies an office, acts are seen as nonpersonal and as continuing over time, across different actors. (pp. 728-729)

Zucker found that extent of institutionalization exhibited the expected effects: Subjects working in more institutionalized conditions were more likely to transmit the standards they had learned in an initial series of trials (with the confederate supplying the standard) to a new naive subject; maintain their standards over time (subjects were asked to return one week later to perform the same type of activity); and resist attempts to change their judgments (having adopted the confederate's standard in the initial period, subjects were exposed to a second confederate who attempted to alter the standard).

Note the extent to which the experiment is built on a cognitive conception of institutionalization. The only factor manipulated to account for the repetitive behaviors of the subjects was their cognitive framing of the situation, including their own identity within it. No sanctions or other types of regulative controls were involved in producing the observed effects. In a recent postscript, Zucker (1991) argues that her experiment draws attention to the microfoundations of institutionalization and that a focus on cognitive measures at the organizational level in contrast to legal rules and resource flows at the macro- or environmental level helps to differentiate institutional arguments from being confounded with resource-dependence arguments.

Boeker (1989) studied factors affecting the institutionalization of power differences present at the time of founding in a sample of 53 semiconductor companies. He examines factors associated with the development of certain configurations of subunit power as well as factors associated with the maintenance or institutionalization of these differences over time. For present purposes, only the latter are of interest. Difference scores were employed to evaluate changes in subunit power between the time of founding and the time of the study. Boeker reports that companies that performed better, were younger, and whose founding entrepreneurs had longer tenure were more likely to retain the power differences established at the time of their founding.

Process Approaches to Diffusion

The diffusion of an institutional form across space and/or time has a dual significance in institutional analysis. On the one hand, diffusion of a set of rules or structural forms is often taken as an indicator of the extent or the *strength* of an institutional structure. Thus, in this sense, studies of institutional diffusion may be regarded as studies of increasing institutionalization. On the other hand, because the diffusing elements are being adopted by or incorporated into organizations, studies of diffusion are also properly treated as studies of institutional effects. In such studies, early or later adoption is often argued to follow different principles because of the changing strength of the institutions. I discuss studies emphasizing adoption in Chapter 5.

Two types of process approaches to the study of institutional diffusion are considered: the ecological and the infrastructural.

In a bold theoretical gesture, Carroll and Hannan (1989a; see also Hannan and Carroll 1992) propose that the density of an organizational form—the number of organizations of a given type—can be interpreted as a measure of the legitimacy of that form: of the extent to which the form is institutionalized. They argue that organizational density serves as an indicator of the cognitive status of the form, the extent to which it is taken for granted, and the extent to which "relevant actors regard it as the 'natural' way to organize for some purpose" (Carroll and Hannan 1989a, p. 525).

Their empirical research, based on studies of seven populations of newspapers, supports their expectation that legitimacy increases monotonically with density, but at a decreasing rate (p. 526). Their explanation for this empirical regularity is that

> rarity of a form poses serious problems of legitimacy. When few instances of a form exist, it can hardly be the natural way to achieve some collective end. On the other hand, once a form becomes prevalent, further proliferation is unlikely to have much effect on its taken-for-grantedness. (Carroll and Hannan 1989a, p. 525)

Mathematical models of the growth rates of the newspaper populations are proposed and evaluated. Subsequently, similar tests have been conducted and confirmed by various researchers in studies of the following kinds of populations: labor unions, semiconductor manufacturers, voluntary social service organizations, wineries, breweries, banks, and life insurance companies.

Critics have raised several questions about this work. Zucker (1989) takes issue with Carroll and Hannan's interpretation on the grounds that their approach does not directly measure legitimacy; however, Carroll and Hannan (1989b) respond that much work in social science involves the modeling of unmeasured variables; moreover, they have examined historical records to document their claim that the first newspapers—the types of organizations on which their study was based—were highly controversial during their founding period. In addition, they assert that one of the strengths of using density as their indicator of legitimacy is its generality: it can be applied to any type of organizational population. Delacroix and Rao (1994) accept

Carroll and Hannan's argument for the validity of density as an indicator of legitimacy for new and somewhat controversial organizations such as newspapers and unions, but suggest that this interpretation is less applicable to more conventional organizations, "especially those involved in business but also nonprofit organizations whose legitimacy is rarely questioned" (p. 260). Singh (1993) points out that although generality is a virtue in any measure, it often is achieved by trading off precision and realism. (These issues are pursued in Chapter 5.)

As discussed in Chapter 3, organizational density is a measure of prevalence or orthodoxy and emphasizes the cognitive aspect of legitimacy: the extent to which an organizational form is taken for granted. Other measures focus on legitimacy that stems from normative support or legal sanction indicating the approval of regulatory agencies or professional associations, such as measures of licensure and certification.[5] Such measures have been employed by Singh et al. (1986), among others. However, because in these studies, institutionalization is employed as an independent variable to examine its effects on organizational populations, I review this research in Chapter 5.

The infrastructural approach to diffusion focuses attention on the characteristics of the diffusion agent and the networks connecting this source to potential adopters. Rather than stressing the nature of the object of diffusion—the new form or innovation—or the characteristics of the adopting units, this view emphasizes the role and connections of the source or the "propagator." As developed by Brown (1981), the infrastructural approach does not replace earlier formulations that examined adopter characteristics (discussed in Chapter 5) but supplements them with information on the strategies of diffusion agencies and their pattern of information flow and influence processes. In economic terms, a supply-side model is proposed to complement the demand-side approach.

Strang and Meyer (1993) have proposed that our understanding of the diffusion of institutional patterns will be better informed if, in addition to examining the relational connections among the social entities involved in these transfers, we take into account the cultural and cognitive connections. They argue, for example, that flows are increased where the actors involved are perceived as similar—"practices diffuse along lines of social relations, but also to other actors broadly considered similar" (p. 492)—when the diffusing practices are theorized as similar, and when the practices are theorized so as to connote modernity. They suggest that "these arguments give importance to legal, and especially professional and scientific, cultural materials. These forms of theorization, and their rise to dominance in the modern world, greatly speed diffusion of rules and practices" (Strang and Meyer 1993, p. 506).

Three empirical studies are employed to illustrate the infrastructural model. In their well-known study of the diffusion of civil service reforms, Tolbert and Zucker (1983) examine the development and diffusion of municipal civil service reform in the United States during the turn of the century, from 1885 to 1935. They contrast two types of diffusion process: the situation in which particular states embraced the reform and mandated that cities under their jurisdiction adopt it and the situation in which a state did not take such action but allowed individual cities to make the decision as to whether to adopt the reform. States mandating the reform used a centralized decision structure and employed legal procedures and official sanctions to enforce compliance. The institutional arrangement was that of a hierarchically structured, regulative system. By contrast, cities in states lacking mandates were responding to a social movement—a cultural model of reform relying on normative influence. Cities in states mandating the reform were much more likely to adopt civil service provisions than those in states lacking such mandates. They did so much earlier and more completely: Mandated reforms were adopted by 60% of the municipalities within a 10-year period, whereas it took 50 years for nonmandated reforms to approach this level of diffusion (Tolbert and Zucker 1983, p. 29).

Tolbert and Zucker argue, nevertheless, that the cultural-normative model of reform was increasingly becoming institutionalized as "the proper way to manage cities" throughout the period under study. As evidence, they report that selective characteristics of individual cities (described in Chapter 6) were predictive of city adoption during the earlier period but, over time, became less and less predictive. They argue that early cities adopted these reforms out of rational self-interest; later, cities adopted them because they wanted to be in conformity to prevailing beliefs.

> As an increasing number of organizations adopt a program or policy, it becomes progressively institutionalized, or widely understood to be a necessary

component of rationalized organizational structure. The legitimacy of the procedures themselves serves as the impetus for the later adopters. (Tolbert and Zucker 1983, p. 35)

However, the *absence* of correlations provides, at best, weak empirical support for the argument. The analysts would be on safer ground to have independent evidence documenting the development over time of a cultural-normative infrastructure.

In her study of profound social change in Japan during the late 19th century during the Meiji period, Westney (1987) provides a historical account of the conscious selection by Japanese officials of selected Western models regarded as successful for organizing particular organizational fields, such as police systems and postal services. These models were then "imposed" on the relevant sectors, employed as a basis for introducing or restructuring existing organizational arrangements. The diffusion of these models exhibited differing patterns, affected by the variable authority of the propagating officials, the presence of relevant cognitive models supplied by indigenous organizations (e.g., the army or the police), and the availability of supporting organizations in the immediate environment.[6]

Cole (1989) examines differences among organizations in Japan, Sweden, and the United States in the adoption and retention of innovative small group activities (such as quality circles). His analysis emphasizes the role played by varying national infrastructures—governmental agencies, trade associations, and union organizations—in legitimating, informing, and supporting the innovation. Japan, more than Sweden, and Sweden more than the United States, created such supportive structures with the result that the innovations have spread more widely and have proved to be more stable in the former than the latter societies. Cole's study represents an advance over previous research in providing independent documentation regarding the existence of the supportive infrastructures of varying strength. Their existence is not simply inferred from information on the diffusion of the practices.

Variance Approaches to Diffusion

A number of recent empirical studies have examined factors accounting for the diffusion of a set of practices through a collection of organizations. Most of these studies emphasize differences among organizations that affect their rate of adoption. These studies, dealing with the organizational effects of institutional pressures, are described in Chapter 5. A few studies emphasize factors that account for why and how some practices rather than others become institutionalized. These studies are our current focus.

Sutton and colleagues (Sutton, Dobbin, Meyer, & Scott, 1994) employ longitudinal data on nearly 300 American employers regarding their adoption during the period 1955-1985 of selected due process protections: disciplinary hearing and grievance procedures for non-union employees. These changes in governance are argued to be responsive to new public policies concerning equal employment opportunity and affirmative action promulgated by federal agencies and courts. These coercive forces became linked to normative pressures "for legalization exerted through the boundary-spanning activities of personnel management professionals" (p. 949) as they interpret and help to craft responses acceptable to judges and related officials (see Edelman [1992] for a related discussion). Analysis revealed that the diffusion of these structures was greatly dependent on governmental pressure: "Rates went up with expanded legal and political pressure in the 1970s and show some signs of having leveled off in the 1980s" (p. 966). Which types of reforms diffused depended on which types of professionals were influential: The diffusion of disciplinary hearings was associated with unionization, whereas the spread of grievance procedures was positively associated with links to human relations professionals but negatively associated with unionization.

Concluding Comment

More attention has been paid by students of organizations to how institutional forces affect organizations than to how institutions themselves arise, persist, and diffuse. These latter questions, however, are garnering increased interest. In reviewing arguments and evidence on the development, persistence, and diffusion of institutions, we have put to work the distinctions developed in Chapter 3. In asking how institutions arise and persist, it matters whether they are conceived to be regulative, normative, or cognitive systems. It also matters how they are carried and the level at which they operate. Another distinction is introduced that pertains more to how questions are posed by the analysts. Some, employing a variance approach, attempt to examine which factors best account for the characteristics or behavior of institutions. Others, employing a process approach, attempt to determine the way in which the factors came together—the sequence, the timing, and the relative power and attention of the actors—to produce the observed result. Both views shed light on how institutions work.

The persistence of institutions, once created, is an understudied phenomenon. Our current understanding of social structures is that their persistence is not to be taken for granted. It requires continuing effort—"talking the talk" and "walking the walk"—if structures are not to erode or dissolve. The conventional term for persistence—inertia—seems on reflection to be too passive and nonproblematic to be an accurate aid to guide studies of this topic.

By contrast, the diffusion of institutional forms over space and time has attracted considerable attention. Diffusion is of interest to the more theoretically oriented as a palpable indicator of institutional strength; to those of a more practical bent, and in a culture emphasizing modernity, change is viewed as progress and adoption of new forms as innovation. Most of the attention to diffusion has emphasized an adoption or demand-side approach. However, an infrastructural or supply-side perspective appears particularly well suited to expanding our understanding of institutional processes. It deserves more consideration.

The most lively current debate in organizational circles involves efforts to evaluate the claim by ecologists that prevalence or density of organizational forms provides a valid and generalized indicator of legitimacy. Critics have challenged the theoretical justification—most preferring a normative model—as well as the empirical evidence. This debate, if nothing else, suggests the utility of differentiating clearly among the extant models of institutions and the varying bases of legitimacy.

Notes

1. In his empirical work on the TVA, Selznick (1949) emphasized the crescive, unplanned, and unintended nature of institutional processes: Valued commitments were generated over time as unanticipated consequences. However, in his later, more prescriptive writing on leadership

(Selznick 1957), he argued for a more intentional model: Effective leaders are those who can define social values and obtain the support of others in preserving them (see Scott 1987).

2. For other examples of process studies employing primarily normative conceptions of institutions, see the discussion of the emergence of various types of international regimes in Krasner (1983) and the related discussion in Mares and Powell (1990). In addition, see Fligstein's analysis of changes during this century in "conceptions of control" negotiated between large diversified companies and the state (also discussed in Chapter 5).

3. For another example of process studies focusing on cognitive aspects of institutions, see Bartunek's (1984) study of changes in the interpretive schemes employed by a religious order together with associated changes in its social structure.

4. This does not imply that institutional processes are only relevant to the retention phase. They also play a significant role in the variation phase (e.g., affecting the cognitive frames in terms of which possible models are defined) as well as in the selection phase (where concerns for attaining legitimacy often dominate which models are retained).

5. Alternative language has recently been proposed by Aldrich and Fiol (1994) to differentiate between these two measures. They propose to call the first, the prevalence indicator, "cognitive" legitimacy, and the second, the normative approval indicator, "sociopolitical" legitimacy.

6. For a related study examining the introduction by Meiji officials of the Western model of the limited liability corporation to structure business and commercial ventures, see Takata (1994).

5 Institutional Effects on Societal Systems, Organizational Fields, and Organizational Populations

Empirical Research

I turn now from the determinants to consider the consequences of institutions and institutionalization. In the studies to be reviewed, institutions are treated as the independent variable or as the force behind the events of interest. Although such studies have been conducted at all levels of analysis (see Table 3.3), I restrict attention to the four levels that have received the most attention from institutional analysts: to the forces shaping societal systems, organizational fields, organizational populations, and organizational structures. The discussion is arranged in terms of level of analysis rather than approach—variance versus process—but I take account of approach in the discussion. In this chapter, effects on societal systems, organizational fields, and organizational populations are discussed. Effects on organizational structures are reviewed in Chapter 6.

The studies of societal systems, organizational fields, and populations reviewed in this chapter testify to the impact of institutional thinking on the study of organizations. The studies of these newer, collective levels of analysis examine the ways that wider and nonintuitive orders of social structure take shape and have an impact on organizational elements and processes. These works exhibit clear connections with the historical traditions described in Chapter 1; however, they have not simply recreated these earlier approaches, but extended them.

Before examining institutional effects at these several levels, however, I begin by discussing two broad types of institutional agents that exercise strong effects at every level: the nation-state and professional occupations.

Institutional Agents: The State and the Professions

DiMaggio and Powell (1983) astutely observe that the state and the professions "have become the great rationalizers of the second half of the twentieth century" (p. 147). In this role, they have come to replace the competitive market that was the early foremost engine of organizational rationalization.[1]

The State

From some perspectives, the state is simply another organizational actor: a bureaucratically organized administrative structure empowered to govern a geographically delimited territory. But such a view is limited and misleading. In our own time (and since the dawn of the modern era), the state has been allocated—is constituted in such a way as to exercise—special powers and prerogatives. As Streeck and Schmitter (1985a, p. 20) point out, the state is not simply yet another actor in the environment of organizations: Its "ability to rely on legitimate coercion" makes it a quite distinctive type of actor. All organizations are correctly viewed as governance structures, but the state is set apart. Lindblom (1977) notes: "The special character of government as an organization is simply . . . that governments exercise authority over other organizations" (p. 21).

Campbell and Lindberg (1990) point out that the state exercises its effects in two distinct ways. On the one hand, the state is correctly viewed as a *collective actor* or, more accurately in the case of liberal states, as a set of semiautonomous actors. State structures vary greatly—among themselves and over time—in their overall strength, in the extent of their unification or fragmentation, and in their degree of federalization: the relative power and autonomy of local, regional, and national bodies (see Abzug and Mezias 1993; Scott and Meyer 1983/1991; Thomas and Meyer 1984).

As collective actors, agencies of the state can take a variety of actions, including granting special charters, allocating key resources such as finance capital or monopoly status, imposing taxes, and exercising regulatory controls. Political scientists and economists have examined the effects of such political controls on industries and firms (see Wilson 1980; Fromm 1981; Noll 1985). The state as a collective actor operates primarily via regulative processes.

Baron, Dobbin, and Jennings (1986) provide a descriptive account of the power of the state to shape industrial and organizational features in their study of the evolution of modern personnel systems in the United States. The strongest evidence of state influence occurred in connection with mobilization for World War II when the federal government intervened to stabilize employment. Agencies such as the War Production Board, the War Labor Board, and the War Manpower Commission "engaged in unprecedented government manipulation of labor markets, union activities, and personnel practices. These interventions . . . fueled the development of bureaucratic controls by creating models of employment and incentives to formalize and expand personnel functions" (Baron et al. 1986, p. 369).

The second way in which the state can affect organizational systems at various levels is as an *institutional structure*. Campbell and Lindberg (1990) identify three varieties of institutional effects. First, the state provides a "distinctive configuration of organizations," the structure of which itself exerts effects on the organizational systems at all levels. For example, Meyer and I (Scott and Meyer 1983/1991) have examined the effects of the fragmentation—multiple competing centers—of authority on organizational fields and structures. Second, as institutional structures, states provide different arenas within which conflicts within and between organizations and systems of organizations can be adjudicated (Campbell and Lindberg 1990). Political scientists Hult and Walcott (1990) provide a useful classification and analysis of a variety of such arenas or forums, ranging from hierarchical to adjudicative and from adversarial to collegial in their structure and modes of actions. Such arenas vary, for example, in where expertise resides, what decision rules are employed, and what forms of participation are permitted. These differences in process, in turn, produce different outcomes. Hierarchies, for example, permit easier access and afford more rapid decisions but often ignore relevant differences among those presenting their case. By contrast, courts pay close attention to the facts and circumstances surrounding particular cases but operate much more deliberately (see Horowitz 1979).

Third, and arguably most important, states have the capacity to "*define and enforce property rights,* that is, the rules that determine the conditions of ownership and control of the means of production" (Campbell and Lindberg 1990, p. 635). Labor laws, for example, affect what rights workers have to take collective action, and antitrust laws limit concentration of ownership. The capacity to create and transform property rights is, of course, just a special case of the power vested in institutions to constitute actors, both individual and collective (see Chapter 3). For economic actors, property rights are among the most fateful and significant rights to be conveyed. As institutional structures, arenas, and definers of property rights, states are exerting primarily cognitive and normative effects on organizations and organizational systems.[2]

The Professions

In different times and places, varying groups control formal knowledge. In some situations they are soothsayers; in others, they are priests; in still other situations, they are intellectuals; but in our own secularized and rationalized times, they are professionals (see Abbott 1988; Freidson 1986; Meyer 1994).

Professionals exercise their control via cognitive and normative processes. More so than other groups, "the professions rule by controlling belief systems. Their primary weapons are ideas. They exercise control by defining reality—by devising ontological frameworks, proposing distinctions, creating typifications, and fabricating principles or guidelines for action" (Scott and Backman 1990, p. 290). The professions construct cognitive frameworks that define arenas within which they claim jurisdiction and seek to exercise control. Simply knowledge in and of itself does not guarantee dominance, as Freidson (1986) and Abbott (1988) have been at pains to demonstrate. Social and political structures must be created and jurisdictional claims defended—often with the aid of the state—if professional power is to be realized.

The interrelations between professional and political actors show exceeding variety and complexity over time and place, but such connections are in evidence for all successful professions. In some instances, the professional associations and practitioners have been so successful early in staking out and defending their jurisdictional claims against competitors that they have been invited to assist the state in exercising control over all providers—both individual and corporate—of designated services. Such is the strong position of the medical profession in the United States (see Freidson 1970; Starr 1982), which is authorized both to exercise controls over a domain in lieu of state power and to share the powers of the state in governing the medical arena. In other cases, the state has been at the forefront of creating a structure of controls that have then been taken over and retained by professionals. This is the situation described by Baron and colleagues (Baron et al. 1986) when employment systems created by state coercion during the crisis of World War II were retained and diffused by a rapidly growing cadre of managerial and personnel professionals.

Although the professions and the state are invariably connected, Meyer (1994) argues that the loose coupling of this connection has consequences. Because many professionals are not located in positions that give them direct authority over the activities they are attempting to influence—and hence they are not held accountable for their proposals—they are more inclined to make recommendations and propose reforms without regard for the availability of resources or the feasibility of implementation. The lack of such accountability, Meyer argues, has led to the rapid proliferation of proposals for rationalizing schemas at every level.

Effects on Societal Systems

Three studies are reviewed to illustrate empirical work examining institutional effects at the societal level, focusing particularly on effects having consequences for organizations. Two of the studies compare institutional structures across two or more societies and examine their effects on economic policies and industrial structure. The studies reviewed are Hall's (1986) examination of the economic governance structure in Britain and France and Whitley's (1992a, 1992b) study of differences in how firms and markets are socially constructed in China, Japan, and Korea. The third study focuses on changes over time in governmental policies and managerial conceptions in a single society in order to evaluate changes in the composition and structure of the largest corporations. This study, by Fligstein (1990, 1991), focuses on historical changes affecting the largest corporations in the United States. All of the studies emphasize the importance of history, attending to when and how developments occurred.

As a historical institutionalist, Hall (1986) employs a relatively broad and loose conception of institutions as including "the formal rules, compliance procedures, and standard operating practices that structure the relationships of people in various units of the polity and economy" (p. 19). His conception is intended to be broader than simply focusing on the formal constitution and structures of the state (as was characteristic of earlier institutionalists in political science), but more restricted than one that deals with the effects of wider cultural norms. His approach encompasses regulative, normative, and cognitive processes. He is concerned to show both how the structures created to formulate and execute policy advantage some types of actors over others, and how location within these structures, "by establishing his institutional responsibilities and relationship to other actors, . . . shapes an actor's definition of his own interests" (p. 19). Thus institutions are seen not only to empower and constrain actors but to constitute them.

Hall examines the general contours of economic policies and policy arrangements in Britain and France (and more briefly, Germany) from the late 19th century to the present, but concentrates on developments since World War I. He attends to five factors shaping economic policy: the organization of labor, the organization of capital, the organization of the state, the organization of the political system (electoral practices and the network of organized political parties), and the position of the nation within the international economy. The institutional arrangement forged by the interaction of these forces "both conditions and reflects the distribution of power" expressed in the economic policies of each society" (p. 232). Hall does not attempt to account for specific policy decisions but rather for the evolution of general economic policy patterns, relating to macroeconomics, industry, and income, distinctive to each country.

In common with most institutionalists, Hall stresses the role that institutions play in imposing a measure of continuity on policy over time, but he also points to instances where institutional arrangements help to contribute to radical political change. For example, in Britain, "the combination of responsible cabinet government and a two-party political system" provides opportunity for radical shifts in policy to attend changes in political power (P. A. Hall 1992, p. 107). This institutional arrangement, Hall argues, facilitated a dramatic shift in economic policy, from Keynesian to monetarist, when Margaret Thatcher came to power in 1979.[3]

Like Hall, Whitley (1992b) focuses on institutional arrangements shaping economic activities: firms and markets. Whitley also takes a relatively broad view in his conception of institutions. He differentiates between more basic or "background" institutions "that structure general patterns of trust, cooperation, identity and subordination in a society" and those "proximate" institutions that are more directly involved in the economic system, including arrangements for obtaining financial resources and labor power together with the "overall political and legal system which institutionalizes property rights [and] provides security and stability . . . for business activities" (Whitley 1992c, pp. 19, 25). The latter are often created as a by-product of the industrialization process itself and frequently developed in association with the formation of the state.

The key dimensions of business systems that Whitley seeks to account for are (1) the nature of firms as economic actors, including the extent to which firms dominate the economy and how they share risks; (2) the nature of authoritative coordination and control systems within firms, including the types of authority exercised and extent of differentiation and decentralization; and (3) the nature of market organization, including the extent of interdependence among firms and the role of competitive versus cooperative ties (pp. 8-19).

In particular, Whitley (1992b) proposes to analyze and explain the

emergence of distinctive "business recipes" in various institutional environments. . . . These business recipes, or systems, are particular ways of organizing, controlling and directing business enterprises that become established as the dominant forms of business organization in different societies. They reflect successful patterns of business behaviour and understandings of how to achieve economic success that are reproduced and reinforced by crucial institutions. (p. 125)

Whitley argues that although social scientists have long entertained a social constructionist perspective in explaining many features of society—from language and kinship structures to stratification systems—they have been reticent to apply these arguments to economic systems, which are treated in a more realist vein. He argues such privileged treatment is unwarranted (for a similar argument, see Calhoun 1990). There is not a single economic logic that disciplines firms: rather, the rules of markets and the recipes for succeeding in them are socially constructed. To demonstrate his argument, Whitley provides a detailed analysis of the important variations that exist in the types of firms—their rights, composition, extent, and modes of interdependence—and in the nature of what is defined as successful and legitimate business practice in contemporary China, Japan, and Korea (see Whitley 1992a, 1992b).[4]

Fligstein (1990) combines both process and variance approaches in examining the transformation of the corporate sector in the United States from the 1800s to the present. He concentrates attention on the 1,000 largest industrial enterprises in the United States, recognizing that the actual organizations making up this set change over the period of study; his quantitative analyses are usually based on the 100 largest firms. The study examines the interdependence over time in state regulatory policies, the nature of organizational fields, conceptions of corporate control, and the structures and strategies of individual firms.

For Fligstein (1990), "the state is made up of the organizations, institutions, and practices that constitute the political function of any given society" (p. 7). Concretely, Fligstein focuses primarily on the regulatory policies of the federal government but also attends to the role of individual states and the courts. Although he views the state as both internally differentiated and a somewhat autonomous social entity whose actors have their own interests, he asserts that, at the time and place of his study, the state generally served the interests of the large firms.

A key construct for Fligstein (1990) is the *conception of control:* "a perspective on how firms ought to solve their competitive problems

[that is] collectively held and reflected in their organizational fields"
(p. 12). He identifies four conceptions of control, each dominant during a different period: the *direct* control conception, post-Civil War to
1904, in which firms engaged in a wide variety of tactics aimed directly
at competitors to reduce competition during the period; the *manufacturing* conception, 1904-1940, in which firms attempted to reduce "in-
terference from competitors by controlling inputs and outputs
through the vertical and horizontal integration of production" (p. 14);
the *sales and marketing* conception, 1940-1970, in which firms focused
attention "on finding, creating and keeping markets" (p. 14); and the
finance conception, 1970 to the present, which emphasizes "control
through the use of financial tools which measure performance according to profit rates" (p. 15). These collectively held beliefs emerge from
the "interaction of leaders of large firms" (p. 12) but must be ratified
by the state, which passes on their legitimacy and legality. Existing
conceptions provide a "solution to the problem of control" and help
"create norms" (p. 20) that guide action within the field; new conceptions are triggered by economic crises or the emergence of new strategies that upset the existing balance of power.
      Fligstein's conception of organizational field reflects aspects of the
conventional definition first proposed by DiMaggio and Powell (1983),
as described in Chapter 3, but also presents some novel features. Like
the more common view, Fligstein (1990) posits that its existence

> is established by the mutual recognition of actors in different firms of their
> interdependence. These actors share a similar conception of legitimate action
> and the place of each organization in that field. The function of organiza-
> tion fields is, first and foremost, to promote stability. (p. 6)

However, having adopted a definition emphasizing the cognitive and
normative facets of fields, Fligstein goes on to recognize their regulative features, stressing the role of power and noting in whose interests
control is being exercised: Organizational fields "are set up to benefit
their most powerful members" (p. 6). It is they who formulate the rules
and have the power to enforce them.
      Also, more than other analysts, Fligstein attends to the transforma-
tion over time of organizational fields. In the early stage of the period
under review, during which direct controls were dominant, a genuine
field, with commonly recognized boundaries and agreement on legiti-

mate modes of action, did not exist. The manufacturing conception of control was associated with the development of fields defined by single products or industries. With the emergence of a marketing conception, definitions of fields broadened to encompass all firms competing in the same markets (with the added complexity that one's competitors and allies varied from one market to another). And with the advent of a financial conception, fields for these large organizations were no longer defined in either product or market terms. "Finance-oriented executives are not committed to any given industry and no longer identify their firms in market terms. Instead, the population of the largest firms is now the reference group for these managers" (Fligstein 1990, pp. 31-32). In short, the field for these organizations is now defined on a societal if not a global level.

Fligstein develops and illustrates his argument by providing considerable historical detail concerning shifting economic policies by the state and changes over time in the composition of the largest industrial corporations, their structure, and their strategy. Quantitative evidence is adduced to show the connection between structure and strategy (e.g., that unified companies are more likely to pursue product-dominant or product-related strategies, whereas multidivisional companies were more likely to pursue diversified strategies; see also Rumelt 1974) and to document the claim that different structures and strategies are dominant during different time periods.

The only systematic data supporting the thesis of changing definitions of field and conceptions of control consist of information on the background of corporation presidents. CEOs were more likely in later than earlier periods to have had experience working in other firms and different types of firms, suggesting a broadening of the boundaries of the field over time. Also, the background specialization of the presidents shifts over time. President's background is employed as an indicator of both "power and perception" (Fligstein 1991, p. 322). During the earliest period the majority were generalist entrepreneurs; during the second period, most came from manufacturing; during the third period, many still came from manufacturing but a large number came from sales; and in the current period, the largest proportion come from finance backgrounds (see also Fligstein 1987).

In a number of respects, Fligstein's arguments are intended to challenge the influential work of the business historian Chandler (1962, 1977), whose earlier analyses attempted to account for the emergence and spread of the unified structural form and its later replacement by the multidivisional form as representing a primarily rational process. Structure follows strategy, and strategy is driven by market pressures for efficiency. Fligstein's account differs in the attention he gives to institutional factors, including the role of the state and the importance of shared beliefs: conceptions of corporate control. But more fundamentally, Fligstein's thesis is that economic markets are themselves shaped by sociopolitical forces. Fligstein (1990) argues that all markets are socially constructed:

> All markets are comprised of a social structure or set of rules which preserves the power and interests of the larger organizations. When the rules no longer produce positive results for those in control, the rules are changed. (p. 303)

These three studies display many similarities and a few differences. All are comparative, across space or time, and all are historical, following the course of events in real time. All give some attention to agency: to human actors pursuing their interests, although Fligstein gives more explicit attention to this dimension than does Hall, and Hall more than Whitley. All are social constructionists: actors may be pursuing their interests, but the actors and their social locations and modes of action are socially constituted as, indeed, are the interests they pursue. Finally, all take a broader rather than a narrower view of institutions, which are seen to have regulative, normative, and cognitive aspects. Moreover, these features do not seem to be in conflict or to undermine each other, as has been argued by some theorists (see Chapter 3). Perhaps, at the macrolevel, where complex institutions such as markets are constructed to stabilize relations and behavior, the use of power and sanctions, up to some point, to reinforce these arrangements does not undermine their cognitive and normative supports. In particular, agencies of the state are constituted in such a manner as to legitimately exercise sanctioning powers.

Effects on Organizational Fields

Most studies of institutional effects have examined social structures specialized around a subset of activities within a single society—either specific types of organizations or organizational fields. As discussed in Chapter 3, the emergence of the concept of organizational field to isolate for analysis sets of differentiated, interdependent organizations that "constitute a recognized area of institutional life" (DiMaggio and Powell 1983, p. 143) has proved to be a valuable source of insights for students of organizations. Organizational fields are often treated as independent variables, affecting organizational forms or processes (see Chapter 6 for examples). Here, however, I consider studies that seek to discover what factors determine the boundaries of fields and the ways in which they are organized, in particular, their governance structures and the extent of their structuration (for an amplified discussion, see Scott 1994a).

Bounding Organizational Fields

As is the case with the definition of populations, most analysts adopt commonsense definitions of fields: a set of diverse organizations attempting to carry on a common enterprise. Although most work on organizational fields assumes a macro to micro ordering—emphasizing the role of the state or professional groups in shaping field definitions—some scholars are asking what role micro processes play in creating macrolevel phenomena (see Lant and Baum forthcoming). These analysts are exploring a cognitive approach to determining the boundaries of organizational fields or subenvironments within which information and influence processes operate. A cognitive lens helps to break down the artificial distinction between organization and environment by recognizing that belief systems exist both objectively, as social "facts" in the cultural environment, and subjectively, as conceptions in the minds of individual participants.

How do organizational participants determine what business they are in, who their competitors are, or from whom they can profitably learn? Porac and Thomas (1990) argue that the structure of an industry not only influences managers' cognitions but is also shaped by managers' cognitions. Abrahamson and Fombrun (forthcoming) encompass these and related questions under the general rubric of macrocultures: the sharing of beliefs among top managers across organizations.

A number of researchers have examined the development of such macrocultures in diverse organizational fields, including Scottish knitwear (Porac, Thomas, and Badden-Fuller 1989), New York hotels (Lant and Baum forthcoming), and iron and steel manufacturers (Stubbart and Ramaprasad 1988). Lant and Baum, for example, examine the ways in which hotel managers categorize other firms as within or outside of their competitive set. They observed how managers selected out a subset of firms defined as relevant in terms of their strategic choices. These firms operated as cognitive communities, exhibiting a convergence of perceptions and beliefs among managers within these competitive groups. These managers appeared to identify firms that were like their own, fairly homogeneous with respect to size, location, and market segment.

Reviewing these and related findings, Abrahamson and Fombrun (forthcoming) suggest that participants' beliefs regarding solidarity or cohesion are more strongly affected by exchange or symbiotic relations, whereas their views of competitive relations are more shaped by structural equivalence: occupying similar positions in a network of relations.

Governance Structures

Governance structures may also arise from influences initiated by more macrosystems (top-down processes) or from forces stemming from their constituent units ("bottom-up" processes). Without question, the single most studied top-down influence on the structure of the governance systems for organizational fields is the state. It is obvious that governance systems for the society as a whole will influence governance systems for subunits in that society. What is perhaps less obvious is the great variety of mechanisms and arrangements employed to govern different fields in the same society. This diversity has come to be recognized, somewhat to their surprise and, perhaps, dismay, by political scientists conducting comparative research on national political organization. For example, a collection of political scientists, sociologists, historians, and economists studying "the institutional structure of capitalism" under the auspices of the Social Science Research Council have discovered that

> despite the apparently homogenising effect of a burgeoning world capitalist system (and, perhaps, even because of it), the practices of capitalism are becoming more, not less, diverse within national economies, at the same time

that they are becoming more similar across national economies. (Schmitter 1990, p. 12)

Sectors, or fields, have been found to vary greatly in their governance structures—ranging from the more spontaneously equilibrating operation of markets to various types of self-enforcing mechanisms, such as alliances or network forms, to externally enforced hierarchies and regulative structures (see Cawson 1985; Kitschelt 1991; Peters 1988; Wilks and Wright 1987). Such arrangements may arise and be sustained by the actions of members of the field or they may be imposed by rule and sanction by "authorities" from above; most often, some combination of both will be at work. For example, in their study of the evolution of governance regimes in industrial sectors, Campbell and Lindberg (1991, p. 328) argue that actors within the sector engage in a process of "constrained selection," involving negotiations between producer organizations, other organizations (suppliers, labor, financial institutions, and consumers), and state organizations. Together with their colleagues, they examine these processes in detail for selected U.S. industries such as telecommunications, the steel industry, and the nuclear energy sector (see Campbell, Hollingsworth, and Lindberg 1991).

Regulative activities vary greatly in their scope. Wholey and Sanchez (1991) note that economic policies are more likely to be sector specific, whereas social policies, such as employment opportunities or occupational safety controls, tend to be applied more broadly across sectors. Among policies aimed at a specific sector, Barnett and Carroll (1993b) distinguish between particularistic regulations, targeted for some subset of organizations in the field, and universalistic policies, aimed at the entire community of organizations in the field. They argue that the former are more likely to produce unintended effects, as, for example, was the case when particularistic attempts to reduce the power of AT&T triggered unexpected competition between large and small independent telephone companies (Barnett and Carroll 1993a).

Viewed as an institutional structure, the modern liberal state is highly fragmented, composed of collections of semiautonomous agencies and sovereigns. This configuration can itself have effects on organizational fields. For example, Meyer and I (Scott and Meyer 1988), employing a variance approach, compare the structure of governance mechanisms of public and private schools in the United States and argue that much of the elaboration and complexity of the former is due to the fragmentation in public authority exercised over public schools. A related study demonstrates that the administrative complexity of public school structures, including state, district, and individual school levels, has increased over time as a function of the growing number of non-coordinated federal educational programs (Meyer, Scott, and Strang 1987).

Campbell and Lindberg (1990) argue that "the state may manipulate property rights in different ways in different sectors of the economy and this will influence governance regimes in these sectors accordingly" (p. 635). The state has used this power to intervene, in different ways, in industries as varied as rail transportation, nuclear power, steel, and telecommunications (see Campbell et al. 1991; Barnett and Carroll 1993b; Dobbin 1994).

Field Structuration

Giddens (1979)[5] defines *structuration* quite broadly to refer to the recursive interdependence of social activities and structures. DiMaggio and Powell (1983) borrow the term but define it more narrowly as referring to the degree of interaction and the nature of the interorganizational structure that arises at the level of the organizational field. Among the indicators they propose to assess structuration are the extent to which organizations in a field interact and are confronted with larger amounts of information to process, the emergence of "interorganizational structures of domination and patterns of coalition," and the development of mutual awareness among participants in a set of organizations that they are involved in a common enterprise (DiMaggio and Powell 1983, p. 148). To these indicators others can be added, including extent of agreement on the institutional logics guiding activities within the field, increased isomorphism of structural forms within populations in the field, increased structural equivalence of organizational sets within the field, and increased clarity of field boundaries (Scott 1994a). Three studies examining field structuration are reviewed.

In his analysis of organizational fields defined by organizations devoted to the arts (theaters, orchestras, and museums), DiMaggio follows Bourdieu (1975) in emphasizing the field as signifying both common "purpose and an arena of strategy and conflict" (DiMaggio

1983, p. 149). He proposes and evaluates the proposition that the more centralized the resources on which organizations in the field depend, the greater the structuration of the field. His empirical study examines the effect on the arts field of the centralized resources created by the establishment of the National Endowment for the Arts (NEA) in the United States in 1965. DiMaggio describes how interaction among the various arts organizations increased, in part because of NEA's efforts to solidify its constituency, but also because diverse types of organizations were now competing for the same resources. New layers of public bodies were created at the individual state level to process the block grants, and new trade associations were created and dormant ones restored to life. Coercive, mimetic, and normative (as well as competitive) pressures led to increased isomorphism among arts organizations in their internal structure. Receipt of federal funding by some but not all applicants tended to increase the legitimacy of successful enterprises and the dominance and centrality of their managers. DiMaggio provides little systematic data to support his arguments, but illustrates the types of data that are relevant.

A study by Meyer and colleagues (Meyer, Scott, Strang, and Creighton 1988) examines changes in the field of public elementary and secondary education in the United States occurring during the period 1940-1980. Employing data collected from the universe of school and district organizations, the authors provide considerable evidence of increasing structuration as schools and districts are shown to become more similar over time in size and internal staffing characteristics. However, unlike DiMaggio's study, which emphasizes the effect of centralization of funding, Meyer and colleagues report, based on both cross-sectional and longitudinal analyses of states, no consistent effects of centralized state or federal funding on structuration. Rather than signifying the impact of the power of centralized state control systems, the authors suggest that increased structuration reflects a process of societal rationalization. They find no evidence for a unified organizational center but rather the "classic" U.S. pattern of "a profusion of professional standards, court decisions, special-purpose legislative interests, and a huge network of interest groups"—a strong polity and lively civic culture (p. 165). The structuration of education "reflects a growing national institutional structure, but not one controlled by the central bureaucratic state" (p. 166).

Laumann and Knoke (1987) have carried out an ambitious study comparing the relative organization and operation of the field of organizations involved in the setting of U.S. national policy in two arenas, health and energy, at the end of the 1970s. In an imaginative approach, Laumann and Knoke employ network techniques to examine the interrelation of organizations, both private and public, of issues, and of organizations activated by issues. They argue:

> Because a specific policy event is embedded in the context of other antecedent, concurrent, and impending events, we must systematically consider the unfolding structure of organizational participation as it is embedded in a structure of events that are tightly or loosely coupled because of institutional, substantive, and historical considerations. (Laumann and Knoke 1987, p. 39)

Organizational location in a policy arena is mapped in terms of core/periphery (relational ties) and interest differentiation (issue involvement). Of principal interest here is the comparison between the degree of structuration of the two fields. Laumann and Knoke argue that at the time of their study, the health policy arena was much more highly structured with well-established scientific and professional organizations operating from early in this century. By contrast, for most of the 20th century, policies on energy had been fuel specific such that only quite recently has a unitary arena for energy policy emerged. Their systematic data confirm this conclusion: "In contrast to the health policy domain during the late 1970s, activity related to energy issues was marked by fragmented participation, enduring conflicts, and a lack of consensus concerning the distribution of influence within the domain" (Laumann and Knoke 1987, p. 72). It appears that the length of time an organizational field has been in existence affects the stability and coherence of its structure.

Effects on Organizational Populations

A promising development in organization theory is the growing convergence between ecological and institutional approaches to organizations (see Hannan and Freeman 1989; Singh and Lumsden 1990). Although these literatures developed as quite independent approaches, since the mid-1980s there have been fruitful interchange and overlap in theoretical frameworks. Because ecological theorists deal primarily with factors affecting the growth and decline of populations of organizations,[6] it did not take long for them to become aware of the effect on these processes of institutional environments.

I described in Chapter 4 the treatment by ecologists of organizational density as an indicator of legitimacy, in particular, the extent to which the form is taken for granted. This approach, in effect, treats this aspect of institutions as an effect of ecological processes: taken-for-grantedness as a consequence of density or increasing prevalence. However, ecologists are also interested in examining the effects of increased density on population processes. As reported in Chapter 4, a sizable number of empirical studies have shown that density is related in a nonmonotonic manner to organizational mortality: Death rates of organizations decrease as density increases up to some point, determined empirically, where competitive pressures overtake institutional supports, causing death rates to increase (see Hannan and Carroll 1993). New populations grow slowly because the form is suspect, unconventional; particular organizations exhibiting the new form are less likely to survive. But to the extent that such organizations do survive and the prevalence of such organizations increases, the form becomes accepted as natural, and new instances enjoy improved survival rates. This result, however, may reflect not only these cognitive supports but also vicarious learning effects and the assistance received from an increasingly elaborated infrastructure of supporting organizations (see Delacroix and Rao 1994).

The density approach emphasizes the cognitive aspects of institutions. Other research by ecologists has focused attention on the effects of various normative aspects of institutions, in particular, endorsement of the legitimacy of an organization by external authorities in the form of licensure or certification. Such measures have been employed by Singh et al. (1986) to examine the impact of registration by a state agency and listing in a community directory on the survival chances of voluntary social service organizations in Toronto, Canada. Event history models are employed to demonstrate that organizations receiving such endorsements of their legitimacy were significantly more likely to survive during their early years, overcoming the "liability of newness" (Stinchcombe 1965) and eliminating the effect of age on mortality rates.[7] In a related study, Baum and Oliver (1991) found that child care service organizations in Toronto were more likely to survive if they had multiple institutional linkages—for example, connections to governmental regulators, service contracts with metropolitan agencies, and site-sharing arrangements with other community organizations—and if they adopted a not-for-profit organizational form than were organizations lacking these connections and assuming a for-profit identity. Again, event history analysis procedures were employed to model these effects over time.

In a reanalysis of their data on day care centers, Baum and Oliver (1992) contrast the effects of "population density" and "relational density"—the latter referring to the "number of linkages between the DCC [day care center] population and the dominant institutions in the environment that confer resources and legitimacy" (p. 547). When population density was evaluated without taking into account relational density, results showed the expected effect on founding and failure rates: Increased population density had legitimating effects at lower levels, increasing founding and reducing failure rates, but at high levels competitive effects dominated, reducing founding rates and increasing failure rates. However, when relational density was taken into account, the legitimating effects of population density were attenuated, so that founding and failure rates were competitive over the entire range of the variable. Moreover, individual organizations with such environmental linkages—which provide both legitimacy and tangible resources—were more likely to survive than were organizations lacking such supports. Baum and Oliver conclude that, at least for this type of social services population of organizations, institutional linkages that embed the population in its environment provide more palpable support than does increasing prevalence of the form.

In addition to examining cognitive and normative effects of institutions on organizations, researchers have also examined the effects of regulative processes: legitimacy that stems from being legally mandated or sanctioned. Regulative facets of institutions are conventionally assumed to affect the behavior of targeted organizations, but recent studies by ecologists indicate they can also affect their life chances. For example, Hannan and Freeman (1989) report that the founding rate for labor unions increased significantly during the New Deal period, 1932-1947, when the Norris-LaGuardia and the Wagner Acts gave increased legal protection to unions and union-organizing campaigns. Similarly, a study of Manhattan banks and U.S. insurance companies found the onset of state and federal regulation to be strongly and positively related to increases in the size of the two populations (Ranger-Moore, Banaszak-Holl, and Hannan 1991).[8] Although empirical studies have yet to be conducted, Wholey and Sanchez (1991) have offered a series of interesting hypotheses detailing the range of potential regulative effects on populations, including their impact on ease of entry of firms into markets, the diversity of firms within a market, effects on population growth dynamics (the rate of growth or decline of populations), effects on the carrying capacity of the environment, and effects on the level of competition between populations.

Other researchers have examined the effects of the institutional structure of the state on population dynamics. For example, in a series of studies, Carroll and colleagues (Carroll and Delacroix 1982; Carroll and Huo 1986; Carroll 1987) found that political turbulence (political events evoking intense reactions) was positively associated with the foundings of newspapers in Argentina, in Ireland, and in the San Francisco Bay Area. They also report that newspapers founded during these periods were more likely to fail. Disruptions in the state institutional framework appear to have consequences for the life chances of at least certain types of organizations.

Carroll, together with Barnett (Barnett and Carroll 1993a), has also examined the effects of fragmentation in state authority—the existence of many semiautonomous units attempting to exercise state authority—on the number of telephone companies operating in the United States during the early years of this century. At that time, telephone companies were subject to local community control. Barnett and Carroll found that the larger the number of political units issuing charters, the larger the number of telephone companies in existence in these areas. More generally, Carroll, Delacroix, and Goodstein (1988) offer a wide-ranging collection of propositions linking characteristics of political environments—including political turmoil, revolution, war, regulation, and institutional structure—to various aspects of organizational populations. Many of these arguments have yet to be evaluated empirically.

Finally, it is possible to view the very existence of a population as resulting from institutional processes. Although they provide no empirical support for their arguments, Hannan and Freeman (1989) have suggested the value of viewing the definitions of populations and the boundaries separating one from another as institutionally

constructed. They argue that processes involving both external legitimation and cognitive codification

> operate on any sort of initial diversity, transforming arbitrary differences
> into differences with real social consequences. . . . They become real in their
> consequences when they serve as bases for successful collective action, when
> powerful actors use them in defining rights and access to resources, and
> when members of the general population use them in organizing their
> social worlds. Thus, the clarity of a set of boundaries is not a permanent
> property of a set of classifications. Rather, the realism of distinction among
> forms depends on the degree of institutionalization that has occurred.
> (Hannan and Freeman 1989, p. 57)

This conclusion reached by two macro-ecological theorists surprisingly resembles the views, as summarized above, of micro-cognitive
theorists as both attempt to understand the social processes involved
in bounding organizational fields and populations.

Concluding Comment

Much of the attention of institutional theorists has been devoted to
examining the effects of institutions on social life at the macro-,
societal level. Such studies have long been the stock-in-trade of historical institutionalists as they have examined the effects of varying
rules, beliefs, and legal requirements on social structures and practices. In particular, much effort has correctly been directed to documenting the role of the state and the professions in promulgating and
enforcing institutional requirements. Surprisingly, however, it is only
relatively recently that much attention has been directed explicitly to
examining such institutional effects on the organizational realm.

Supplementing the longer term efforts to examine societal-level effects, more recent work has concentrated on examining institutional
effects on organizational fields and on organizational populations. As
DiMaggio (1986) asserts: "The organization field has emerged as a
critical unit bridging the organizational and the societal levels in the
study of social and community change" (p. 337). Wider societal forces
operate to structure organizational fields, which develop their own
distinctive cultural beliefs and governance systems, and these systems,
in turn, structure individual organizations.

Institutional effects are also being examined at the level of the organizational population. Population identities and boundaries between populations are themselves the product of ongoing constitutive processes that act to "blend and segregate" varying organizational forms over time. Recent research has examined the effect of legitimacy—defined in the cognitive sense of prevalence of the form, in the normative sense of being morally endorsed or certified, and in the regulative sense of being legally sanctioned—on organizational vital rates: foundings and failures. Although effects have been observed for all three modes of legitimacy, it remains to be determined how these forces interact and for which types of populations each mode is most salient.

Notes

1. Note that the market is more properly treated as a set of rules or conventions than as a collective actor: a social agent.

2. For a related discussion that focuses more explicitly on the legal aspects of state power, see Scott (1994d).

3. Dobbin (1994) has conducted a related study focusing on societal differences in economic policies. His focus is on policies affecting the emergence of the railroad industry in the United States, Britain, and France. However, in his approach, Dobbin places more emphasis on the importance of cognitive factors—institutionalized meaning systems and political cultures—shaping economic policies than does Hall.

4. In related work, Biggart, Hamilton, and colleagues (Hamilton and Biggart 1988; Orru, Biggart, and Hamilton 1991; Biggart and Hamilton 1992) have closely studied the institutional underpinnings of three East Asian economies—Japan, South Korea, and Taiwan—examining how the various network forms constituted in these settings differ from each other as well as from Western models of corporate organization.

5. Giddens (1979, 69-76, 1984) replaces the noun *structure* with the verb *structuration* to stress that structures are systems of ongoing action, being continuously produced and reproduced through time. The concept also emphasizes the "duality of structure: the mutual dependence of structure and agency," as discussed in Chapter 3.

6. As Carroll (1984) has noted, ecological arguments can be applied at the level of the individual organization, the organizational population, or the organizational community (multiple interacting populations). I restrict attention here to the population level.

7. Event history methods blur the distinction between variance and process studies. Variables are identified but the analysis procedures take into account both changes in the value of independent variables and the timing of such changes (see Tuma, Hannan, and Groeneveld 1979; Tuma and Hannan 1984).

8. However, when density dependence was taken into account, these effects were substantially reduced. The researchers propose that rising density may "drive the process of initial government regulation, not the reverse" and that growth in numbers may also signify strength of the industry, allowing it to "influence authorities to take actions that favor the interests of those organizations and their elites" (Ranger-Moore et al. 1991, p. 63).

6 Institutional Effects on
Organizational Structure
and Performance

Empirical Research

M ost research on institutional effects by organizational scholars has
focused on the effects on individual organizations. In this chapter, I review representative examples. Early studies tended to emphasize the effects of institutional context on all organizations within the
relevant environment. The institutional environment was viewed as
imposing structures on individual organizations who were required
to conform, either because it was taken for granted that this was the
proper way to organize, because to do so would receive normative appro-
bation, or because it was necessary in order to obtain resources. Later
studies began to emphasize individual differences among organizations: Whether and how organizations responded depended on
their individual characteristics or connections. Recent theorists and
researchers have stressed the varied nature of organizational responses

to institutional demands. In some cases, the demands themselves are negotiated, as organizations collectively attempt to shape institutional requirements and redefine environments. In other cases, individual organizations respond strategically, either by decoupling their structures from their operations or by seeking to defend themselves in some manner from the demands. I review examples of these sets of studies.

Structural Effects
of Institutional Context

Stinchcombe (1965) was the first organizational theorist to emphasize the importance of the social (including institutional) conditions present at the time of the founding of the organization on the organization's structure. Such "imprinting" effects are important because they tend to persist—to become institutionalized. Stinchcombe provides data on differences in the labor force composition of varying industries to illustrate this effect, demonstrating that industries founded in different periods tended to exhibit differing labor force characteristics and that these differences were maintained over time. Kimberly (1975) evaluates the imprinting argument at the organizational level by studying a collection of 123 rehabilitation organizations (sheltered workshops) established in the New York region from 1866 to 1966. During the latter part of this period, the beliefs and norms pertaining to these workshops shifted from an emphasis on the production of goods and services for its community to a focus on the psychological rehabilitation of the clients. Whereas only 18% of the workshops founded before 1946 were rehabilitation oriented, 64% of those founded after that date exhibited this orientation. Moreover, the later in the period studied at which a workshop was founded, the more likely that a rehabilitation orientation would be chosen. Although this study does not systematically assess changes in the cognitive models and norms governing these organizations, it is clear that the more recent organizations differed substantially from earlier forms in their orientation and internal characteristics.

In his study of semiconductor firms described in an earlier chapter, Boeker (1988) also contrasts the impact of entrepreneurial and environmental effects at the time of the firm's founding on current firm strategy. He finds that the previous functional background of the entrepreneur influenced the selection of the firm's strategy, but also that this decision was independently influenced by the industry's stage of development at the time the firm was founded. Firm strategies were significantly affected by industry stage in three of the four stages examined. For example, firms founded during the earliest era were more likely to continue to pursue first-mover strategies, whereas firms founded during the most recent period studied were more likely to pursue a niche strategy.

Gradually, both theorists and researchers have come to realize that although organizations confront and are shaped by institutions, these institutional systems are not necessarily unified or coherent. A variety of researchers have explored the effects on organizations of environmental complexity, instability, and inconsistency (see Brunsson 1989; Meyer and Scott 1983b; Zucker 1988a).

Several researchers have examined the effect of institutional complexity on organization structure. For example, Meyer and I (Scott and Meyer 1983/ 1991) propose that organizations confronting more complex, fragmented environments—for example, multiple authorities and/or funding sources—would develop more complex and elaborated internal structures, holding constant the complexity of their work processes. Powell (1988) finds evidence consistent with this prediction in his study comparing a scholarly book publishing house and a public television station. He concludes that "organizations, such as [the public television station] WNET, that are located in environments in which conflicting demands are made upon them will be especially likely to generate complex organizational structures with disproportionately large administrative components and boundary-spanning units" (Powell 1988, p. 126).

Meyer and colleagues (Meyer et al. 1987), in a study described in an earlier chapter, employ data on the administrative structure of districts, elementary schools, and secondary schools to demonstrate that schools and districts depending more on federal funding, which involves many independent programs and budgetary categories, had disproportionately large administrative structures compared to schools relying primarily on state funding, which tended to be more integrated. However, testing this proposition on a random sample of agricultural cooperatives in Hungary, Carroll and colleagues (Carroll, Goodstein, and Gyenes 1988) report findings opposite to those predicted: Cooperatives reporting higher levels of fragmentation in decision making within the system of public organizations having influence over them had lower administrative ratios than those reporting more integrated decision systems. The authors speculate that this unexpected finding may result from the fact that the cooperatives are not really independent firms in this socialist state: "If so, then the administrative work of a cooperative may actually be lessened because it is absorbed and conducted by the state agencies" (Carroll et al. 1988, p. 254). In any case, a socialist state clearly constitutes a different kind of institutional structure than those presented by capitalist systems, as Burawoy (1985) has demonstrated.

Other studies have focused on the consistency of support for institutional rule systems and prescribed routines. Thus Rowan (1982) studied the adoption and retention of three administrative innovations by a random sample of city school districts in California during the period 1930-1970. These programs were shown to have varying degrees of support from influential institutional agents—legislatures, professional associations, and teacher-training institutions. Rowan's study finds that programs enjoying more consistent, balanced support from these agents were more likely to be adopted and to be retained than programs lacking such support, after taking into account district size and complexity. This is one of the few studies that attempt to address the important questions: What determines which institutional models will be adopted and which will be retained by organizations? (For a relevant discussion, see Abrahamson 1991.)

D'Aunno and colleagues (D'Aunno, Sutton, and Price 1991) examine effects on community mental health organizations exposed to two conflicting models for staffing and providing services in drug abuse programs. The conventional mental health approach prescribed a psychosocial model of treatment administered by mental health professionals, whereas the competing model, more common in the drug abuse treatment sector, endorsed the Alcoholics Anonymous model, relying on ex-addicts and client-centered approaches. As some mental health centers, termed "hybrids," elected to treat drug abuse cases, they were confronted with the two conflicting institutionalized models of treatment. The results show that hybrid organizations reflected the conflicts in their environments by attempting to incorporate some features consistent with both the mental health and the drug abuse institutional practices. These organizations "responded by combining hiring practices" from the two sectors; "hybrid units also adopted conflicting goals for client treatment and somewhat inconsistent treatment practices" (D'Aunno et al. 1991, pp. 655-656). Conflicts in the environment were reflected in the structure and practices of these organizations.

Interaction Effects

Although all organizations within a given institutional field or sector are subject to the effects of institutional forces within the context, all do not respond in the same manner to these pressures. Just as social psychologists call our attention to individual differences—differences among individuals in their definition of and response to the same situation—students of organization increasingly have attended to differences among organizations in their response to the "same" environment. I review here studies examining how responses vary because of differences among organizations in their characteristics or in their location within the field. In a later section of this chapter, I consider how responses vary because organizations are reacting strategically to their situations.

In Chapter 4, I reviewed several studies examining the diffusion of an institutional practice among organizations. At that time, the interest was in viewing diffusion as an indicator of increasing institutionalization. Now I turn the attention to how diffusion is affected by the characteristics not of the propagator, but of the adopting organization.

I begin by revisiting the Tolbert and Zucker (1983) study of the diffusion of civil service reforms among municipalities at the turn of the century, portions of which were reviewed in Chapter 4. Considering just those states in which civil service was not mandated, Tolbert and Zucker show that its adoption by cities during the initial period varied according to their characteristics: Larger cities, those with higher proportions of immigrants, and those with a higher proportion of white-collar to blue-collar inhabitants were more likely to adopt the reform. The authors argue that these cities were behaving rationally in pursuing their own interests: Local governments were adopting changes that would buffer them from "undesirable elements" and link them to "better" segments of the community. City characteristics were strongly predictive of adoption during the first period (1885-1904) but in each subsequent period became weaker, so that by 1935, they no longer had any predictive power. The authors interpret these weakening correlations as evidence for the development of increasingly widespread and powerful cultural norms supporting civil service reform such that all cities were under increasing pressure to adopt the reform regardless of their local needs or circumstances. Although this is an interesting and plausible interpretation, it suffers from two problems. First, it ignores the possibility that cities were also undergoing change during this period, with the result that different, unmeasured city characteristics were causing some cities to adopt the reform, whereas others, lacking these features, did not (see Scott 1987). Second, as noted in Chapter 4, the authors provide no independent measures of the growing strength of cultural norms supporting reform. Without such evidence, their arguments remain plausible, but unsupported, conjectures.

Tolbert and Zucker (1983) assume that "as an increasing number of organizations adopt a program or policy, it becomes progressively institutionalized" (p. 35).[1] Although they do not use this information as a direct measure of institutionalization, other analysts have done so. For example, Fligstein (1985) tests a number of alternative arguments for why large firms adopted the multidivisional (M-form) structure. His data were collected at five periods, each a decade from 1929-1939 to 1969-1979, and included information on the 100 largest U.S. industrial corporations for each period. During the earlier periods, firms that were older, pursuing product-related strategies in their growth patterns, and headed by managers from sales or finance departments were more likely to adopt the M-form than firms lacking these characteristics. During the 1939-1949 period, these same factors continued to operate, but another variable also became relevant. If firms were in industries in which other, similar firms had adopted the M-form, they were more likely also to adopt this structure. Fligstein interprets the variable—number of adopters in the industry—as measuring mimetic pressures on the firm to imitate the practices of their competitors. All of the factors, with the exception of age, continue to be significantly correlated with M-form adoption during the last two decades included in the study (for an earlier, related study reporting similar results, see Rumelt 1974).

Fligstein's study provides empirical support for two different versions of institutional arguments. The findings linking structural forms to strategies support Williamson's (1975) arguments that organizational managers attempt to devise governance structures that will economize on transactions costs. The findings relating M-form adoption to number of other similar firms employing the structure are consistent with DiMaggio and Powell's (1983) views of mimetic processes operating in uncertain environments. The former arguments are typically treated as reflecting a rational course of action, whereas the latter are treated as nonrational. However, without information on the effect of these decisions on performance measures, it is not possible to make this determination (for other studies of the diffusion of structural reforms, see Knoke 1982; Burns and Wholey 1993; Zhou 1993).

Other studies have examined variation in organizational response to normative or regulative pressure as a function of organizational characteristics related to their vulnerability, visibility, or location in the field. Mezias (1990) reports a study of changes in the financial reporting practices of the 200 largest nonfinancial firms in the United States for the period 1962-1984. A modification in accounting procedures for reporting the income tax credit was recommended by the professional body, the Accounting Principles Board (APB). Although most of the firms adopted the new procedure when the APB lifted its prohibition against it, other organization-level factors also affected acceptance of this normatively sanctioned practice. Firms that were under the jurisdiction of the Interstate Commerce Commission were more likely to adopt the new practice than those that were excluded from oversight by this regulatory body. And firms that experienced a changeover in their top-management team were more likely to adopt the new practice. Mezias (1990) suggests that the latter effect may be interpreted as reflecting "the diffusion of normative models by supplying personnel who have experience with practices that are widespread but not yet adopted by the focal organization" (p. 442). Although Mezias does not directly test this relational explanation, other researchers have tested similar arguments, which I review below.

A related study by Greening and Gray (1994) examines variation in organizational structures developed to respond to social and political pressures in their environments. Organizations operating in three industries—utilities, petroleum and gas, and food processing that varied in the extent to which they experienced crises or controversies—were surveyed to determine the degree to which managers had devoted specialized attention and resources to management of these issues. Environmental turbulence (both perceived and objectively measured) predicted level of resources committed by organizations but not other structural responses. Organizational size was associated with both increased formalization of issues management and the commitment of resources. Larger organizations were thought to be more visible targets for political activists as well as to possess the scale to support more differentiated structures.

In a series of studies, Dobbin and colleagues (Dobbin, Edelman, Meyer, Scott, and Swidler 1988; Dobbin, Sutton, Meyer, and Scott 1993) and Edelman (1990) attempt to account for differences among two diverse samples of organizations in their adoption of various employee protections, including due process, equal opportunity, and affirmative action procedures. These organizations are viewed as responding to changes in their legal environments that, as Edelman (1990) argues, include not simply changes in legal rules but changes in the broader normative climate that often accompany changes in the law: "The legal environment can engender significant change in the protection of employees' rights, even in the absence of any legal rules that directly mandate such change" (p. 1403). In their study of 52 organizations located in the San Francisco Bay Area, these authors report that nonunion grievance procedures were adopted rapidly after the passage of the 1964 Civil Rights Act, even though they were not legally mandated. Larger organizations, public organizations, and organizations with a stronger link to the public sector—federal contractors—were more likely than smaller or private organizations were to adopt these reforms and to do so earlier. And organizations with more departments with personnel functions and those establishing personnel offices after 1965 were also more likely to adopt grievance procedures (Dobbin et al. 1988; Edelman 1990). The authors interpret organization size as not only measuring the scale and complexity of the organization but also its visibility to external constituencies and, hence, vulnerability to the legal environment. Similarly, public organizations and federal contractors are viewed as being in closer proximity to the public sphere, the seat of legal order. Personnel offices are viewed as important boundary-spanning structures that mediate between the organization and the larger environment. I comment further on these processes below.

A number of the studies just reviewed have implicitly argued that a firm's connections to other firms may have important effects on its behavior. Several recent studies have directly tested this possibility. In his study of factors that influence U.S. corporations to adopt the "poison pill" defense against hostile takeovers, Davis (1991) evaluates several relational arguments. He suggests that "interlock network centrality"—the extent to which members of the corporation's board of directors serve on other corporate boards—signifies the extent to which board members view themselves as part of a corporate elite that acts to prevent the instabilities associated with hostile takeovers. Davis also argues that such ties will be especially supportive of poison pill adoption if the links are to corporations that have already adopted the poison pill. Also, he includes information on the number of similar firms—firms in the same industry—that have adopted this defense. Davis tests these and other arguments on data obtained from 440 of the firms in the Fortune 500 largest industrial companies in the United States for 1986. The data set contained information on all adoptions of the poison pill from the first adopter in 1984 up to 1989, when approximately 60% of the firms had adopted this defense. Event history analysis revealed that the first two variables were strongly predictive of adoption of the poison pill. The greater the centrality of a corporation's board in terms of linkages to other corporations, and the more of these linkages were to other corporations that had already adopted the poison pill defense, the more likely a corporation was to itself adopt this strategy. The third measure, prevalence of adoption by other corporations in the industry in general, was not associated with corporate adoption (for a related study showing the effect of director interlocks on a firm's decision to grow by acquisition, see Haunschild 1993).

This distinction—between what other firms my firm has contact with versus what other firms like mine are doing even though I lack direct contact with them—has become important to network scholars. The former, referred to as *cohesion,* pertains to the presence of exchange relations or communication between two or more parties. The latter, termed *structural equivalence,* refers to social units that "occupy the same position in the social structure"; they "are proximate to the extent that they have the same pattern of relations with occupants of other positions" (Burt 1987, p. 1291). In situations where information is widely available, for example, via the mass media or social contagion, the diffusion of some practice or structure may be more influenced by the behavior of those we regard as similar to ourselves than by those with whom we are in contact.

The relative importance of cohesion versus structural equivalence is evaluated in a study by Galaskiewicz and Burt (1991), examining factors affecting contagion or diffusion of norms and standards for not-for-profit organizations seeking donations among contributions officers in 67 corporate firms. They evaluate how a normative system operates within an organizational field affecting how individual officials come to view their environment, share standards, and arrive at similar evaluations. Results were based on evaluations made by 61 contributions officers of 326 local not-for-profit organizations eligible to receive donations from corporations. Judgments by officers (as to whether they recognized the not-for-profit organizations and, if so, regarded them as outstanding) were correlated with the evaluations of other officers who were either in contact or in equivalent structural positions. "The results show weak evidence of contagion by cohesion and strong evidence of contagion by structural equivalence" (Galaskiewicz and Burt 1991, p. 94). Differences in judgment were also influenced by differences in the personal characteristics of officers, such as gender and prominence, but these did not eliminate the structural effects.

If organizations tend to imitate other organizations like themselves, there remains the question as to how they make this judgment. By what criteria and via what processes do organizations determine the boundaries of their field and the identity of their reference set? (Some studies by cognitive theorists related to this question were reviewed in Chapter 5.) Here, as a final example of a study of organizational differences, I consider the research by Haveman (1993) on decisions by firms to enter into new markets. This study differs from others reviewed in this section by focusing attention not on the characteristics of organizations' choosing but on the characteristics of organizations' being chosen as a reference group. Haveman combines ecological and institutional approaches in her analysis of decisions by 313 California savings and loan companies to enter new markets opened up by deregulation during the period 1977-1987. She treats the decision of an existing firm to enter a new market as equivalent to the decision of an entrepreneur to found a new market, arguing that population density pressures—both legitimating and competitive—should apply to both cases. But the question is, how should the boundaries of these new markets be defined? Haveman assumes, first, that organizations will be likely to imitate organizations within their own population, which she operationalizes as being in the same industry. Within this category, however, how are specific models to be emulated chosen? Haveman evaluates two possibilities: (1) organizations imitate other organizations that are similar to them in size, and (2) organizations imitate others that they regard as more successful, in this case, either the most profitable firms or the largest firms.

Her event history analysis examines factors affecting rates of entry into the new markets by the savings and loan companies. She reports little support for the argument that fields (markets) are defined on a size-specific basis. However, there is fairly consistent support—in four of the six markets studied—for the proposition that organizations imitate other organizations that are viewed as successful: either profitable or large firms. Haveman (1993) also reports an interaction between the characteristics of choosing and chosen organizations: "I found that large organizations serve as especially strong role models for other large organizations but that highly profitable organizations serve as role models for all organizations, not just other profitable organizations" (p. 622).

Collective Responses to Institutional Environments

In spite of the title of their book, *The External Control of Organizations,* Pfeffer and Salancik (1978) devote as much attention to the ways in which organizations defend themselves from various external control attempts as to detailing the various sources of external influence. Oliver (1991) is correct in her charge that early institutional theorists too readily assumed that organizations confronted by external institutional demands have no option but to comply. She argues that this presents too oversocialized and passive a conception of organizations (for similar criticisms, see Perrow 1986; DiMaggio 1988). I agree with Oliver's general criticism and will use her typology of organizational responses, but I want to both conditionalize and then amplify her arguments.

First, the condition: Although it is important to recognize that organizations may react to institutional pressures in a number of ways, it is also important to recognize the extent to which institutional environments influence and delimit what strategies organizations can use.

Just as institutions constitute organizations, they also constitute what are their appropriate ways of acting, including acts that are responses to institutional pressures. Strategies that may be appropriate in one kind of industry or field may be prohibited in another. Tactics that can be successfully pursued in one setting may be inconceivable in another. Not only structures but also strategies are institutionally shaped.

Second, to amplify Oliver's arguments, although she usefully details a number of alternative, strategic responses that are available to organizations facing external institutional pressures, her discussion is restricted to strategies pursued by individual organizations. These are important and will be reviewed below, but equally important are responses made by multiple organizations, responses that have the potential to shape the nature of the demands and even to redefine the nature of the field. I review several studies that have dealt with these collective responses to institutional environments.

Chapter 4 reviewed a number of empirical studies of the ways in which organizations were able to collectively create an institutional framework, for example, colleges developing the National Collegiate Athletic Association or the financial investment companies creating the Chicago Board of Trade. Closely related to these situations are ones in which organizations subject to some type of normative or regulative regime respond in ways that reshape or redefine these institutional demands. I suspect that these processes—in which rules or normative controls are proposed or imposed, reacted to by the organizational field to which they are directed, and then redefined—are more often the rule than the exception.

Miles (1982) has described the interesting case of the response by the "Big Six" tobacco companies in the United States to the Surgeon General's report linking smoking and cancer. Each of these companies reacted individually, some developing their foreign markets and others diversifying their products. But they also engaged in collective action, creating the Tobacco Industry Research Committee to conduct their own scientific studies and cooperating in hiring lobbyists and creating political action committees (PACs) to influence legislation and resist the passage of punitive laws. These interactive efforts to shape the regulative structure to which they are subject continue up to the present day.

In a somewhat similar study, Kaplan and Harrison (1993) examine the reactions by organizations to changes in the legal environment that exposed board members to a greater risk of liability suits. Corporations pursued both proactive strategies, adapting to conform to environmental requirements, and reactive strategies, attempting to alter environmental demands. Both involved collective as well as individual efforts. The Business Roundtable, a voluntary governance association, "took the lead in coordinating the conformity strategy by making recommendation on board composition and committee structure" consistent with the concerns raised by such regulatory bodies as the Security and Exchanges Commission (p. 423). Proactive collective strategies included lobbying efforts directed at states to broaden the indemnification protection for outside directors as well as the creation of insurance consortia to underwrite the costs of providing director and officer liability insurance to companies. The strategies pursued were highly successful: "New legislation and the insurance consortia enabled most corporations to substantially improve director liability protection. As a result, most board members are less at risk of personal liability now than they were a decade ago" (pp. 426-427). There now exists a substantial body of research by social scientists regarding the processes by which firms subject to state regulation work collectively, often through trade associations, to influence both laws and enforcement mechanisms (see, e.g., Wilson 1980; Noll 1985).[2]

Edelman (1992) points out that laws vary greatly in clarity and so in the opportunity they present to organizations for negotiation.[3] She argues:

> Laws that contain vague or controversial language, laws that regulate organizational procedures more than the substantive results of those procedures, and laws that provide weak enforcement mechanisms leave more room for organizational mediation than laws that are more specific, substantive, and backed by strong enforcement. (Edelman 1992, p. 1532)

In later research following that previously discussed, Edelman (1992) and Dobbin and colleagues (Dobbin et al. 1993) describe the response of U.S. organizations to equal employment opportunity/affirmative action (EEO/AA) legislation during the period 1964-1989. Edelman emphasizes how organizations tended to respond to such demands by structural elaboration: creating new departments or offices responsible for compliance. This response is discussed in more detail in the following.

Dobbin and colleagues describe how personnel professionals played a central role in constructing formal compliance mechanisms. These professional actors devised a variety of approaches to compliance, which were then tested by the courts. Varying mechanisms were developed, described, and debated in professional forums, including conferences and personnel journals. One set of proposals, involving job ladders, employment tests, and quota schemes, resulted in reverse-discrimination suits and negative court opinions. Others, involving job descriptions, performance evaluations, and salary classification systems, proved acceptable to the courts. Once these rulings by state officials became clear, then the approved practices diffused rapidly throughout the organizational field. Ambiguous requirements were clarified over time by a negotiation process involving professional personnel officers and educators, on the one hand, and agents of the state, specifically federal judges, on the other.

A different kind of negotiation process and redefinition of the organizational field is described by Halliday and colleagues (Halliday, Powell, and Gransfors 1993) in their study of state bar associations in the United States. These associations began to be formed at the turn of this century as market-based organizations, competing for the support of lawyer members. However, during the early decades, failure rates were high. A different model of organizing was developed in the early 1920s that relied on state support: Membership in the association was mandated as a condition for practicing in the state, and annual fees were imposed on all members. This new form, which required either legislative action or a ruling by the state supreme court, rapidly diffused through a number of states although it did not supplant the market-based form in all states. Event history analysis revealed that the state-based mode was more likely to be adopted in states in which the market-based form had attracted only a small proportion of lawyers, in states that were favorably disposed to licensing professions, and in rural states. The state-based form was also promoted by a centralized, propagator association, the American Judicature Society, created to promote legal reform and diffuse the new structure. Collective action in this case resulted in the transformation of an organizational form, moving it out of the competitive marketplace and under the protective wing of the state.

Responses by Individual Organizations

Focusing attention on the variety of responses available to individual organizations, Oliver (1991, p. 152) identifies five general strategies: *acquiescing, compromising, avoiding, defying,* and *manipulating* (see also Goodstein 1994; Kaplan and Harrison 1993). The first, acquiescence or conformity, is that emphasized by most institutional theorists. The alternative, compromise, which involves balancing, placating, and negotiating with institutional representatives, is particularly likely in conflicting environments. Research on organizations operating in these circumstances was described earlier in this chapter.

Avoidance, disguising one's nonconformity or attempting to buffer parts of the organization from the impact of the demand, is a strategy that has received considerable attention. In their seminal piece on institutions and organizations, Meyer and Rowan (1977) argue that whereas tight coupling of structure to activities is useful for organizations rewarded for their technical performance, organizations responding to institutional demands are better served if they decouple structures from activities. This argument is based on the assumption that institutional rules often conflict with technical requirements or that the institutional rules are themselves in conflict. With respect to the first type of conflict, Meyer and Rowan argue that conformity to institutional rules has ritual significance that maintains appearances and helps to validate the organization but whose costs cannot be justified by technical criteria. Also, institutional rules are couched at high levels of generalization and are often inappropriate to specific situations. For example, a state agency may mandate a curriculum that makes little sense for a particular school.

As to the conflict between institutional rules, Meyer (1983, 1994) argues that one of the major forces shaping modern society is the movement toward increased rationalization, fueled in particular by the growth of science, the professions, and state power. However, as the societal structure becomes more rationalized, the structure of particular organizations becomes less rational: Organizations are expected to reflect in their own structures the multiple, and often competing, bases of rationality present in the wider society.

My own view of these processes is somewhat more moderate. In both cases, I believe that the arguments are not primarily theoretical but need to be resolved by empirical evidence. That is, the extent to which there is conflict between institutional and technical rules or, more accurately, between procedural and outcome requirements should not be asserted but assessed. More specifically, if organizations confront both output and procedural demands, then it is rational (as well as practical) to respond to them, and organizations often do so by differentiating: by developing specialized units equipped and empowered to deal with each type of demand. Loose coupling between differentiated units is a characteristic feature of all organizations, indeed of all open systems (see Glassman 1973; Weick 1976; Orton and Weick 1990). Organizations in particular are recognized as dealing with external demands by developing specialized administrative units (Thompson 1967). Meyer and Rowan suggest that these responses are often merely symbolic, the organizational equivalent of "smoke and mirrors" (see Perrow 1986). I disagree. First, to an institutionalist, the adjective *merely* does not fit comfortably with the noun *symbolic*. Symbolism, the mechanism by which meanings are shaped, exerts great social power (see March and Olsen 1989). Second, numerous studies suggest that although organizations may create boundary units for symbolic reasons, these structures have a life of their own. Personnel employed in these units often play a dual role: They both transmit and translate environment demands to organizations but also represent organizational concerns to environmental agents (see Taylor 1984; Peterson, Rabe, and Wong 1986). And the existence of such units signals compliance. Edelman (1992) elaborates this argument with respect to organizational response to EEO/AA requirements:

> Structural elaboration is merely the first step in the process of compliance. Once EEO/AA structures are in place, the personnel who work with or in those structures become prominent actors in the compliance process: they give meaning to law as they construct definitions of compliance within their organizations. . . . But while actors within organizations struggle to construct a definition of compliance, structural elaboration signals attention to law, thus helping to preserve legitimacy. (p. 1544)

To this point, we have very few studies of the relation between structural and behavioral conformity in response to institutional pressures. One recent study by Westphal and Zajac (1994) examines the behavior of 564 of the largest U.S. corporations in adopting and actually implementing long-term CEO compensation incentive plans.

They find that a large number of such corporations adopted such plans but that a much smaller number actually put them to use. Nearly half of the companies in their sample adopted the plans but made no use of them during the subsequent 2-year period. Moreover, although adoption of the plan was positively associated with CEO influence over the board, failure to use the plan was negatively related to CEO power.

One final comment on Meyer and Rowan's discussion of the conflict between technical and institutional rules: Their discussion appears to focus exclusively on the normative or regulative aspects of institutions, even though much of Meyer's work stresses the cognitive. To the extent that institutional rules constitute the organization, as Meyer argues (see Meyer et al. 1987), specifying the actors and their interests and capabilities and the criteria of effectiveness, then how is it that technical processes are necessarily in conflict with institutional requirements? All technical systems are grounded in institutional environments (see Scott 1987; Powell 1991), so conflicts should not be regarded as automatic or inevitable. A study by Goodstein (1994) regarding factors affecting decisions by corporations to adopt child care services reveals that a number of organizations perceived important technical benefits associated with these programs—for example, improving recruitment and retention; reducing absenteeism, tardiness, and stress; and fostering employee morale and loyalty—and adopted them for these reasons, as well as because of existing institutional pressures.

With respect to conflicts among institutional requirements, there is no question but that many competing and inconsistent institutional logics exist in modern society (see Friedland and Alford 1991). However, the presence and extent of such conflicts remain to be evaluated empirically. The extent to which decoupling, dissemblance, and other forms of avoidance are practiced would be expected to vary depending on whether the demands stem from sources regarded as possessing legitimate authority or from sources thought to be exercising unauthorized power (see Scott 1987).

A fourth strategy identified by Oliver (1991) is defiance. Defiant organizations not only resist institutional pressures to conform but do so in a very public manner. Defiance is likely to occur when the norms and interests of the focal organizations diverge substantially from those attempting to impose requirements on them. Covaleski and Dirsmith (1988) provide a process description of an organization's attempt to defy the state's efforts to impose a budgetary system on them. The University of Wisconsin system attempted to devise and obtain public support for an alternative budgetary system that would reflect more clearly its own interests in research and educational programs and retaining top-flight faculty. In the end, state power prevailed, and the university was forced to accept the more traditional enrollment-based approach.

Fifth, organizations may respond to institutional pressures by attempting to manipulate—to co-opt, influence, or control the environment (Oliver 1991, p. 157). Numerous researchers, from Selznick to Pfeffer and Salancik, have examined the ways in which organizations attempt to defend themselves and improve their bargaining power by developing linkages to important sources of power. Of special interest to institutional theorists are the techniques used by organizations to manipulate views of their legitimacy. Elsbach and Sutton (1992) report a process study of impression management techniques employed by Earth First! and ACT UP, two militant reform organizations that employed "illegitimate actions to gain recognition and achieve goals" (p. 702). Their analysis suggests that such techniques were employed to gain media attention for the organization and its objectives. Once such attention is forthcoming, spokespersons for each organization stressed the conventional aspects of the organization and attempted to decouple their organization's program from the illegal activities of some of its members. They also sometimes claimed innocence or justified their actions in light of the greater injustices against which they were contending. Endorsements and support received from other constituencies are emphasized. In these and related ways, organizations attempted to manage their impressions and improve their credibility. However, as Ashforth and Gibbs (1990) point out, organizations that protest too much run the risk of undermining their legitimacy.

Concluding Comment

Although organization analysts early embraced an open systems conception of organizations, it has taken a long time for them to begin to comprehend the extent to which organizations are creatures of their distinctive times and places, reflecting not only the technical know-how but also the cultural rules and social beliefs in their environments.

As Schrödinger (1945) observed in his treatise on open systems: "The device by which an organism [or organization] maintains itself stationary at a fairly high level of orderliness . . . really consists in continually sucking orderliness from its environment" (p. 75).

Much of the important work by institutional theorists over the past two decades has been in documenting the impact of social and symbolic forces on organizational structure and behavior. Empirical research has examined how institutional systems shape organizations, variably, as a function of their location in the environment, their size and visibility, nearness to the public sphere, structural position, and relational contacts.

Organizations are affected, even penetrated, by their environments, but they are also capable of responding to these influence attempts creatively and strategically. By acting in concert with other organizations facing similar pressures, organizations can sometimes counter, curb, circumvent, or redefine these demands. And collective action does not preclude individual attempts to reinterpret, manipulate, challenge, or defy the authoritative claims made on them. Organizations are creatures of their institutional environments, but most modern organizations are constituted as active players, not passive pawns.

Notes

1. This is the same argument adopted later by the population ecologists in which they propose that organizational density, the prevalence of organizations of a given type, could be used as an indicator of legitimacy: the taken-for-granted status of the form (see Carroll and Hannan 1989). It is somewhat ironic that Zucker (1989, p. 542) in commenting on this usage, criticizes Carroll and Hannan for lacking a direct measure of legitimacy.

2. National political systems vary greatly in the arrangements by which regulative regimes are crafted. Corporatist states incorporate representatives of private interests directly into governance structures, legitimating more involvement of these groups in both rule making and rule enforcement. More liberal states such as the United States emphasize more adversarial and arms-length relations between private interests and state structures (see Cawson 1985; Streeck and Schmitter 1985b).

3. Additional opportunities—and challenges—are afforded to organizations confronting conflicting or fragmented authorities. Abzug and Mezias (1993) detail the range of responses pursued by organizations responding to court decisions regarding comparable worth claims under Title VII of the Civil Rights Act of 1972. The federalized structure of the court systems, allowing for quasi-independent rulings by federal, state, and local courts, provided for a greater variety of appeals but also provided avenues for due process reform efforts to continue at one level when they had been blocked at another.

7 Accomplishments, Continuing
Controversies, New Directions

Accomplishments

Although all movements ebb and flow, the interest in institutions has, during the past two decades, swelled into a sizable flood of work, both theoretical and empirical. And there is no sign of diminishing interest. Even through any assessment may be premature, I believe the work produced to this point shows evidence of substantial positive fruits.

One of the signal accomplishments of institutional analysis is that it has refocused attention on knowledge and rule systems. These "cultural" frameworks attracted the attention of earlier generations of social scientists but were defocalized by later theorists who concentrated on resources and exchange processes external to the organization and on behavior and attitudes within it. Resource dependence and contingency theory emphasized the importance of the technical features of environments. And within organizations, analysts were concentrating on explaining informal structures and individual behavior and attitudes.

Neo-institutional views call attention to cultural and normative frameworks in the environments of organizations and to formal governance structures within them. Organizational structures are argued to have importance apart from—regardless of—their impact on participant behavior. The structures are viewed as signaling purposefulness and rationality internally but especially to external audiences—as demonstrating the organization's connections to and congruence with wider belief and rule systems. Formal structures—constitutions, corporate forms, rule systems, charters, and governance systems—are once again proper subjects of scientific study.

Another of the major contributions of institutional theory to this point is that it constitutes an important bridge linking the social and behavioral sciences. More so than with many intellectual movements, the interest in institutions crosses all the social sciences. Institutional theory and research are flourishing in economics, political science, and sociology and are increasingly forging links to cognitive and social psychology. Within management studies, institutional analysis has captured the interest of both micro and macro students of organizations, organizational economists, and increasingly, students of strategy and of international management.

It is largely because of the institutionalists that economists have become enlisted in the study of organizational structures. Rather than treating organizations only as "black boxes"—as places within which economic transactions take place—an increasing number of economists are beginning to accept the premise that "organization form matters" (Williamson 1985, p. 274): The structural features of organizations, the specifics of their governance structures, affect economic processes and outcomes. Similarly, political scientists are again taking into account the distinctive features of political structures and are examining how the particular characteristics of legislatures, agencies, and committees affect political processes and outcomes. And sociologists who earlier had moved beyond informal networks to investigate formal structures have been emboldened to examine their connection to wider rule systems.

Yet another contribution of institutional arguments is that their development is associated with the emergence of a new level of analysis. To an increasing extent, sociologists, political scientists, economists, and management scholars have begun to recognize the importance of organizational fields. Students of markets, of industries, and of societal sectors are beginning to focus on these intermediate systems that mediate between societal structures and individual organizations, and there appear to be promising signs of cross-fertilization and conjoint learning. The definition of field is, to a large extent, coterminous with the application of a distinctive complex of institutional rules. Because such rules define—constitute and control—much of the activity within the field, analysts are wise to be cautious in generalizing across fields. But we need to understand fields precisely because they constitute somewhat distinctive worlds, operating under different rules, with different logics and different kinds of players.

For similar reasons, the resurgence of interest in institutions has generated renewed interest in comparative studies. Rather than assuming that all organizations are alike, or when differences are found between organizations situated in varying social and cultural contexts, attempting to understate them or explain them away, current work is more likely to celebrate diversity and seek to account for the reasons why different forms arise (see Lincoln 1990; Scott 1991; Biggart and Hamilton 1992).

Because of institutional arguments, the research community has shown new awareness of the importance of history and of process. There is increasing recognition that time matters. Time matters in two senses (see Zald 1990). First, context changes over time, and the particular context within which an organization or wider organizational system develops and operates affects what it does and how it does it. Thus, like comparative studies, historical studies help to make us aware of and inform us about the importance of institutional context. The renewal of interest in institutional theory has both stimulated more analysts to undertake historical research on organizations (e.g., Fligstein's (1986, 1990) research on the evolution of corporate forms) and encouraged scholars to pay more attention to the historical research that has been conducted (e.g., Chandler's 1962 research on the history of corporations).[1]

Second, time matters in that each institution and organization has its own history, its own time-dependent line of development; and how a social system develops and operates affects its structure and capacities for action. Institutionalization is a process occurring over time that can affect what structures develop and persist. An interest in institutionalization has encouraged longitudinal studies of particular organizations and of organizational fields (e.g., Selznick 1949; DiMaggio 1991).

A final indicator of development and progress is the broadening of application of institutional ideas and arguments, which are now being applied and tested across the full range of organizations. In the earlier work, there was a tendency to regard institutional organizations as a subclass of organizations, usually protected from market pressures, lacking a clear technology, and producing outputs whose quality could not be evaluated. Such organizations exist—they include systems such as schools and social service agencies—and it is important to understand how they function as organizations, but it is a serious mistake to assume that these organizations are the only type subject to institutionalization processes and effects. *All* organizations are institutionalized organizations. This is true both in the narrower sense that all organizations are subject to important regulative processes and operate under the control of both local and more general governance structures, as well as in the broader sense that all organizations are socially constituted and are the subject of institutional processes that define what forms they can assume and how they may operate legitimately. Recent theories encompass the full range of organizations, and empirical research is no longer limited to the study of public and other nonmarket forms but embraces all manner of for-profit firms, including multidivisional and multinational corporations as well as the newest models of network or alliance organizations.

Hence institutional theory has stimulated the study of more kinds of organizations, broader collections of organizations, organizations operating in different places and time periods, and changes in organizations and organizational systems over time. Each of these extensions enhances our understanding of organizations. And each connects organizational studies more firmly and fully to the broader agenda of the social sciences.

Continuing Controversies

In Chapter 3, I pointed to two controversies regarding the explanation of institutional forms. The first concerns whether a social constructionist or a social realist position is to be embraced. A second concerns whether the decisions regarding institutional arrangements are to be regarded as guided by rational considerations or a broader conception of practical action. To these two controversies may be added a third, to which I have alluded in previous chapters. This is the question of whether institutions are constructed primarily from the bottom up through the actions of participating actors or whether they are strongly shaped by external, top-down forces. Let us take stock of each.

Social Constructionism and Social Realism

The most profound basis for disagreement among contemporary students of institutions is whether a social constructionist or a social realist position is taken. Social constructionists embrace the most far-reaching and all-encompassing version of institutions: Institutions are seen as constituting the rules, defining the players, and framing the situations. The interests and identities of the principal actors are socially defined and expected to vary across place and time.

At the opposite extreme, a social realist assumes that actors have interests and capabilities by virtue of their innate nature, that human nature is stable across situations and through time. Because actors pursue their private interests in the company of others, whose interests may be in conflict with their own, they come to realize the necessity of constructing at least a minimal frame of rules as the basis for supporting transactions. Because of differences among individuals in interests and power, governance systems with the power to sanction are required to maintain social order.

A more modest difference, but one that has fueled much of the recent renaissance of interest in the study of institutions, pertains to whether the institutional systems and controls are thought to be more cognitive or normative in character. Whereas earlier theorists emphasized the normative features of institutions, the new institutionalists give greater attention to the cognitive features. In the normative view, controls are exercised by the evaluative expectations of others, who communicate prescriptive and proscriptive signals to one another based on their respective positions and on the situation. The more highly institutionalized these expectations, the more widely they are shared by all participants in the situation, and the more likely each participant is to internalize them, applying them to his or her behavior even in the absence of significant others. The cognitive view gives more attention to the understandings and conceptual beliefs shared by those in the situation. Much of behavior is explained in terms of the individual's need to make sense of the situation and to appear as a competent actor within it. As situations become more highly institutionalized, individuals accept and follow social scripts, routines, and performance programs—because they are accepted as "the ways things are done by persons like me in situations like this."

These differing assumptions and perspectives have significant effects on institutional theory and research, creating many of the fault lines around which controversies occur. Because they rest on different views of the nature of social reality—on differing ontologies—they are not likely to be quickly or easily put to rest. I suggest in the next section, however, one basis for resolution. I also call for more research on the elements of institutions.

Rational and Practical Action

Rationality has been defined in a great many ways, but in the organizations literature it generally is viewed as instrumental behavior taken in order to reach desired ends. Rationality is typically defined from the standpoint of the actor, not the observer. In its more extreme version, it is restricted to "the conscious maximization of an explicit objective . . . within the constraints of well-defined alternatives" (Langlois 1986a, p. 6). Later, more relaxed versions regard maximization as too strict a criterion, settling for an acceptable or "satisficing" standard, as well as recognizing that individual action is always constrained by individual limits of information and restrictions in cognitive, information-processing capacities (see Simon 1957; March and Simon 1958). It is this latter, broader version of rationality that is accepted by most rational choice theorists working in the institutionalist arena (see Abell forthcoming).

However, for other scholars, this conception of how choices are or should be made is still too restricted. They embrace a practical model of reasonable or "adaptive" action (see Langlois 1986b, p. 230). These scholars follow March and Simon's argument that, particularly when one is working within an organizational framework where work is subdivided and activities must be coordinated if they are to be effective, making individual choices based on local knowledge can be irrational and following rules or routinized performance programs, sensible. In addition to pointing to the necessity of coordinated activities, these scholars also argue that such routines frequently embody learning from past experiences and evolutionary survivals from previous trial-and-failure efforts (see Nelson and Winter 1982). March and Olsen (1989) embrace and extend this point:

> To say that behavior is governed by rules is not to say that it is either trivial or unreasoned. Rule-bound behavior is, or can be, carefully considered. Rules can reflect subtle lessons of cumulative experience, and the process by which appropriate rules are determined and applied is a process involving high levels of human intelligence, discourse, and deliberation. (p. 22)

Note that March and Olsen suggest that following rules and making choices are not necessarily incompatible. Early institutional formulations sometimes implied that in the usual case, there was one and only one set of unified cultural rules to be followed in a given situation. More recent scholars recognize that in many if not most cases, multiple and sometimes conflicting rules exist. Individuals must therefore decide which rules apply in a given situation. As March and Olsen (1989) note, "the number and variety of alternative rules assure that one of the primary factors affecting behavior is the process by which some of those rules, rather than others, are evoked in a particular situation" (p. 24). The presence of conflicting rules opens up room for individual discretion, for strategic behavior, and for choice. As Swidler (1986) observes, this interpretation of cultural rule systems "should lead us to expect not passive 'cultural dopes,' but rather active, sometimes skilled users of culture whom we actually observe" (p. 277).

The practical model of action also takes into account the fact that we are social beings and that an important aspect of any social situation is taking into account the opinions and expectations of others with whom we are interdependent. Social norms and values are essential ingredients of any social situation; behavior is guided not only by natural endowments and interests but by moral beliefs and normative obligations.

As I have observed, the most generous vision of institutions is that which views these systems as not simply defining the broader context but also constituting the nature of the actors and the possible actions. This social constructionist frame contextualizes rationality; it argues that interests are endogenous and that even our instrumental technologies and our criteria of efficiency are social products. From this perspective, then, who has the right to have interests, what interests are regarded as reasonable or appropriate, and what means can be used to pursue them are all products of socially constructed rules: Institutional rules invent rationality, defining who the actors are and determining the logics that guide their actions. This means that, as the rational choice theorists argue, if actors pursuing interests take actions to create institutional frameworks, this can occur only under particular circumstances in which selected actors are constituted as having these interests and powers. Where social agency is located—who has the right to take self-determined and self-interested actions—is expected to vary over time and place.

Thus rationality is both broadened and constricted by social constructionist arguments. On the one hand, social constructionists broaden the conception of rationality to encompass many, and different, kinds of rationalities. On the other hand, current rational choice models are viewed as applying only under special and limited conditions. The rational choice models apply to only a subset of institutional systems: those that constitute individual social actors as possessing private interests and the capacity to take action to protect them.[2]

Bottom-Up and Top-Down Explanations

In Chapters 4, 5, and 6, numerous studies were reviewed regarding both the construction of new institutions and the transmission or diffusion of existing institutions. The fact that both processes are observed suggests that, at least in some cases, actions viewed by participants and observers as instances of new institutions may in fact represent the copying of an already existing form. Early research emphasized the diffusion of structural forms; more recent work has added organizational strategies.

Sociological observers who emphasize environmental processes—whether coercive, normative, or mimetic—are apt to view the most common institution-forming processes as being top down, emanating from models already existing at societal or field levels. Cultural or structural patterns existing outside of the focal structure—whether field or organization—are seen to be adopted by local participants. A virtue of this perspective is that it helps to account for two widely observed phenomena: the rather limited number of organizational forms found in any given field and the disparity between the "formal" official structure and the actual patterns of work and interaction. If organizations systems were primarily designed by participants within the system to better accommodate the required task performances and interaction patterns, one would expect to see both more variation among organizations and a closer connection between formal rules and actual behaviors (see Meyer and Rowan 1977; Scott 1994c).

Other students of institutional forms emphasize the bottom-up creation of these forms by internal participants. The new institutional economists are apt to view these processes as involving rational design, as entrepreneurs or managers attempt to devise governance structures to improve efficiencies and reduce transactions costs. Many sociological or managerial scholars emphasize the unfolding of a nonrational process in which distinctive cultures are created as an adaptation to particular personalities or as solutions to environmental pressures. The two directional flows linking actors, organizations, fields, and societal forms are illustrated in Figure 7.1.

Figure 7.1 depicts a layered model of institutional forms and flows. Societal institutions provide a context within which more specific institutional fields and forms exist, shaping them both as agent and environment. Organizational fields operate at intermediate levels, providing institutional structures within which specific organizations operate. And organizations provide institutional contexts within which particular actors are located and take action. Generalized models—beliefs, norms, menus, and scripts—flow "down" through the various levels, carried by socialization, social construction, and sanctioning powers. These models are carried and reproduced, but also modified and reconstructed, by the interpretations and inventions of subordinate actors: individuals, organizations, and fields.

Those favoring top-down designs point out the extent to which managers in different situations tend to select the same organizational structures or strategies, suggesting that they are not inventing but borrowing existing models. And the top-down scholars point out to those emphasizing distinctive corporate cultures the extent to which the general concept of a corporate culture is one that appears to be a relatively recent invention and one that is widely promulgated by popular managerial pundits. The particular myths and rituals may be distinctive from organization to organization; what is shared is the

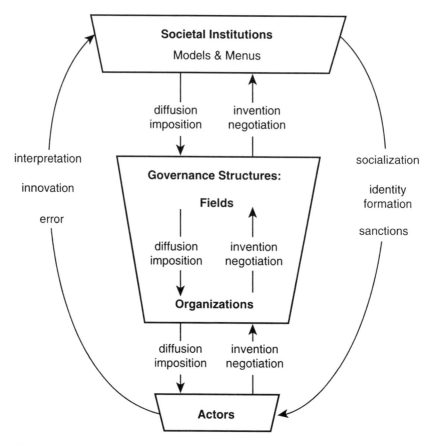

Figure 7.1. Top-Down and Bottom-Up Processes in Institutional Creation and Diffusion
SOURCE: Adapted from Scott 1994c, Figure 3.1. p. 57.

belief that the modern organization must exhibit such trappings. In short, there is considerable evidence of the existence of widespread cultural rule systems and models, not the least of which is the uniformity exhibited by organizational forms operating within the same locations in social fields.

On the other hand, there is also evidence of invention and adaptation by individual organizations. Westney (1987) sets out to tell a story of deliberate cultural imitation as Japanese officials scouted the world for successful models, but the narrative quickly becomes one of cultural invention, as existing ideas had to be fitted into new contexts. Also, as Williamson (1992) argues, all of the models that reside in the wider cultural environment represent creations by particular actors, individual or collective, that others come to regard as successful and, therefore, attempt to copy. Organizational models may be maintained and diffused via processes that operate transorganizationally, but they are regarded by specific organizations' participants as solutions to specific problems.

Edelman (1992) and Dobbin and associates (Dobbin et al. 1993) portray a complex interactive process between the requirements of institutional agents (state officials), on the one hand, and the response of personnel managers who, in both individual and collective ways, devised proposals that eventually resulted in negotiated solutions to meeting equal opportunity requirements. These and the previous examples suggest that organizations and their participants are more active and more involved in developing institutional structures than earlier formulations recognized. Under some conditions, organizational models are produced by interaction and negotiation processes, involving institutional agents and organizational participants.

The controversy over causal direction is one that can be informed by empirical work. There appear to be instances where top-down processes dominate, as seems to be the case with DiMaggio's (1983) description of the structuration of the arts field following the creation of the federal arts program. Suchman's (forthcoming) case of the development of organizational models in Silicon Valley semiconductor firms appears to represent a bottom-up case of institutional construction. Other situations, as noted above in the design of equal opportunity structures, seem to involve complex interactions between organizational and environmental agents (for related discussions, see Meyer 1994; Scott 1994c, Strang and Meyer 1993; Suchman forthcoming).

New Directions

Probing the Pillars

If the pillars framework I developed in Chapter 3 has merit, it should not only be in summarizing and organizing past work on institutions but in raising additional questions to guide the next generation of research. The distinctions I have proposed among the three conceptions—

the three pillars—of institutions are analytical in the sense that concrete institutional arrangements will be found to combine regulative, normative, and cognitive processes together in varying amounts. However, particular institutional forms will vary in their composition, some resting primarily on the regulative, some on the normative, and some on the cognitive pillar. If true, why is this so?

Why are different types of institutions created? Are some types of activities more likely to be governed by one type rather than another? In what circumstances do we construct cognitive frames rather than normative rules to shape and support behavior? Under what conditions do we create governance structures that rely primarily on superior force? Perhaps the type of pillar preferred depends on what types of social actors are involved. Are public agencies and officials of the state more likely to create regulative systems that rely primarily on the legitimate use of power? By contrast, are the normative pillars erected primarily by priests and their modern-day counterparts, professionals—ethicists, reformers, and educators? Are the cognitive pillars constructed by scientists and intellectuals? To be sure, some types of actors have multiple ways of acting. In our own time, lawyers are involved in all three processes acting variously as priests, problem-solving professionals, and agents of the state.

Do these differing types of institutions work in different ways? Certainly, sanctions and expedient responses to them differ from behavior that stems from externalized norms and internalized obligations. And behavior governed by cognitive beliefs and action premises embedded in these beliefs seems more likely to be self-sustaining even in the absence of external constraints. Presumably, also, these institutional forms diffuse in different ways. Cognitive systems may spread by mechanisms quite different from those that support the diffusion of rules. Earlier literature on planned social change recognized that influence attempts based on power and sanctions operated differently and had different effects than those restructuring normative systems or those providing new and different types of factual information (see Chin and Benne 1976).

Are the different types of institutions associated with different carriers? Are the cognitive forms more likely to employ cultural carriers? Are norms more likely to be built into structures or routines?

How do the differing types of institutions fit together? In Chapter 3, I reviewed arguments concerning the incompatibility of the three pillars; how sanctions can undermine internalized obligations and taken-for-granted beliefs. But we also have evidence that in many circumstances, regulative, normative, and cognitive systems appear to be all be present and to operate in mutually supportive and reinforcing ways. How and when is this possible?

I also have suggested that the three pillars may operate at somewhat different levels, with the regulative systems being somewhat more superficial and the cognitive systems working at deeper levels. This suggests a more layered model of institutional controls. Do normative and regulative structures operate within cognitive frames? Do regulative structures also attempt to move toward the creation of a normative base, as Weber suggested?

Are different research methods required to study the different institutional types? Although the regulative and normative types lend themselves to more conventional research methods, it seems clear that we need new and different methods to explore fully the cognitive models of institutions. A number of analysts have pointed to the benefits associated with embracing some types of methods, such as semiotics and narrative analysis, traditionally associated with humanistic scholarship (see Somers and Gibson forthcoming; Zald 1993).

Finally, *how do these varying types of institutions affect the characteristics of organizational fields, populations, structures, and strategies?* We would expect cognitive and normative controls to affect organizational systems more profoundly. These systems rely more on internalization: They get inside the heads of participants, causing them to exercise self- and peer control. Regulative control processes seem more likely to be resisted or to result in only superficial conformity. Are these expectations correct?

Advancing Historical and Comparative Studies

I argued above that a valuable contribution made by institutional scholars to the field of organizational studies (as well as to the social sciences generally) has been to stimulate more historical and comparative research. We need to increase this activity and build on current efforts. The distinctive contribution of comparative and historical studies is that they allow us to vary institutional contexts. It is difficult if not impossible to discern the effects of institutions on social structures and behavior if all our cases are embedded in the same or very similar contexts.

Historical and process studies require different approaches and methods than do studies of comparative statics. In my review of recent empirical research, I noted the increasing extent to which powerful new methodologies are being employed. The analysis of process arguments has been greatly aided by the development of simulation techniques, such as those employed by Axelrod, as well as by the widespread use of dynamic models, such as event history methods (Tuma and Hannan 1984) and techniques for evaluating path-dependent arguments (see David 1988). Other process techniques are under development that need to be appropriated by students of institutions. Van de Ven (1992) has distinguished among different kinds of process arguments—as explanations for variance, as a category of concepts that attempt to capture action, and as developmental sequences of events—and has suggested appropriate methods to describe and evaluate them. And Abbott (1990) has proposed methods that allow analysts to identify characteristic patterns in sequences of events, taking into account not only what events occurred but the order in which they happened.[3]

Case study methods, both qualitative and quantitative, are particularly well suited to the study of social process and have enjoyed a resurgence of interest during the past decade as more analysts ask process questions and attend to how things happen. Qualitative research methods have long been employed in the study of institutional processes (e.g., Selznick 1949). And, recently, more systematic qualitative and quantitative methods have also been used. Such methods have been employed to advantage by, for example, Barley (1986) and Elsbach and Sutton (1992) in examining institutional questions.

With more and better methods, what questions merit attention? First, *we need better information about the life course of institutions.* Although we now have many studies of the emergence of institutions, we have far fewer of the processes by which they persist over time and still fewer of their dissolution. Moreover, virtually all of these studies deal with only one of these phases, either emergence or persistence or deterioration. We need longitudinal studies that capture the entire sequence of institution building, maintenance, and destruction. Such studies can be conducted at the societal level but are probably more manageable at the field level.

Second, *we need studies that focus on the relation between institutional and organizational processes.* Such a focus may be termed "the coevolution of institutions and organizations," paralleling recent studies of the "coevolution of technology and organization" (Rosenkopf and Tushman 1994; Van de Ven and Garud 1994). Such studies benefit by focusing on periods during which new institutional forms are emerging, as in the development of new industries and new organizational forms, or alternatively, on periods during which old institutional arrangements are being delegitimized and new beliefs and rules being constructed.

Dominant approaches to the development of new industries have long emphasized the importance of new, breakthrough, or "competence-destroying" technologies (Schumpeter 1961; Tushman and Anderson 1986). More recent work has emphasized that new industries require the development of a social and political infrastructure that provides working rules, governance structures, and legitimacy. Van de Ven and Garud (1989, 1994), for example, have carried out a study of the construction of new institutional forms associated with the emergence of a new industry, which in turn was triggered by attempts to develop and commercialize the new technology of cochlear implants. In Chapter 4, I reviewed their analysis of the events by which institutional rules were developed and consolidated. In addition, Van de Ven and Garud (1994) connect these processes to others by which an organizational field is created, with a new population of organizations, the devising of industry standards, and the development of a regulatory regime under the Federal Drug Administration (see also Barnett and Carroll's [1993a] study of the early development of the U.S. telephone industry).

In related work, Aldrich and Fiol (1994) have begun to explore the ways in which entrepreneurs operate to actively construct new types of organizations and industries. They distinguish between cognitive and sociopolitical legitimacy, the former referring to the taken-for-grantedness of the new form, products, and emerging relations. They suggest that entrepreneurs can increase the cognitive legitimacy of their operations by using symbolic language and appropriately framing their activities, by encouraging convergence around a dominant product design, and by developing linkages with established educational institutions. Entrepreneurs must also strike some kind of balance between seeking uniqueness as a means of gaining competitive advantage and imitability as a technique for portraying their activities as familiar and trustworthy.

Old institutional forms give way to new ones, a process that presents institutional scholars with another opportunity to better understand the interdependence of institutions and organizations. For example, in the United States, an important institutional change has occurred in the medical care sector during the past two decades with "the coming of the corporation" and the increasingly active role played by federal funding and control agencies (see Starr 1982). Organizational analysts are asking how it was that the earlier professionally dominated governance structures became delegitimated and dislodged (see Alexander and D'Aunno 1990; Scott and Backman 1990). And they are observing the effects of these institutional changes on medical care organizations as traditional service arrangements are broken up ("unbundled"), new more specialized populations of organizations arise, and for-profit firms flourish. Not only are multiple form changes associated with this institutional transformation but both existing and new organizations adapt new competitive strategies of a type that would have been unthinkable under the previous regime (see Fennell and Alexander 1993; Gray 1986; Scott 1993; Shortell, Morrison, and Hughes 1990).

Even more fundamental institutional changes are afoot in other parts of the world—for example, in Eastern Europe and the former Soviet Union, in Western Europe, in Southeast Asia, and in South Africa—as efforts are under way to institute new markets, to support industrial development, and to secure the conditions of democratic government. Institutional scholars must—and many already have begun to—take advantage of these "natural" experiments.

Third, and finally, *we need to do more, and different kinds of, comparative studies.* Comparative studies are particularly beneficial for institutionalists who otherwise are prone to emphasize the uniqueness of their cases. Institutional research can all too readily become institutional history. Although it is true that in their full complexity, every situation is distinctive and unique, a scientific model holds up the value of developing and testing generalizations that apply across time and place. Indeed, institutional theory offers the potential of allowing

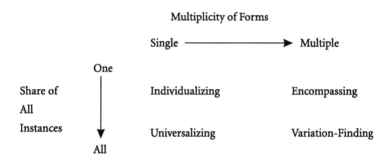

Figure 7.2. Types of Comparative Studies

SOURCE: Tilly (1984, p. 81). Reprinted from *Big Structures, Large Processes, Huge Comparisons*, by Charles Tilly, © 1984 Russell Sage Foundation. Reprinted by permission.

us to combine general arguments with particular conditions—systematic processes with random events—to produce explanations of specific structures.

I believe that the promise of institutional theory is that it enables us to better develop and test what Tilly (1984) refers to as "variation-finding" and "encompassing" propositions. Tilly (1984, p. 81) develops a useful typology of comparative research (see Figure 7.2) by cross-classifying two dimensions: the multiplicity of forms, that is, the number of different kinds of forms studied, and the share of all instances, ranging from the study of one example to all known examples of the form(s). In the individualizing study, the analyst attempts to "contrast specific instances of a given phenomenon as a means of grasping the peculiarities of each case" (p. 82). We compare in order to contrast: to show that the cases differ and how they differ. In the universalizing study, the scholar's interest is to show that "every instance of a phenomenon follows essentially the same rule" (p. 82). The variation-finding study attempts to establish "a principle of variation in the character or intensity of a phenomenon having more than one form by examining systematic differences among instances" (p. 116). And the encompassing study "places different instances at various locations within the same system" (p. 83). That is, this type of study attempts to show not only that the types vary but that these differences are due to theorized and systematic differences in their context or locations within that context.

To illustrate this typology, I return to selected institutional studies already reviewed. Hall's (1986; see Chapter 5) analysis of social policy setting in Britain and France is an attempt to show how these political institutional structures differed and how they resulted in differing policy processes and outcomes. His is an individualizing study. Fligstein (1990; see Chapter 5) provides an example of a universalizing study. His research on the largest corporations in the United States endeavors to show how these corporations over time were responding to similar institutional pressures and moved to adopt similar organizational forms.[4] Davis (1991; see Chapter 6) provides an example of a variation-finding approach as he seeks to account for what types of factors—for example, differences in interlock network centrality—led some corporations to adopt and others not to adopt the poison pill defense against corporate takeover attempts.

I do not think we yet have a clear example of research in the organizations area pursuing an encompassing strategy. However, Jepperson and Meyer (1991) develop (but do not evaluate empirically) a theoretical framework that illustrates this approach. They argue that societies vary in how they organize and locate rationality. Liberal/ individualist societies, for example, the United States, "license individual persons as legitimate and rational social actors," whereas corporatist societies, like Sweden, construct not individual but collective actors ("people and groups as agents performing legitimated social functions"); statist societies, such as France, constitute "pregiven, state-defined, function-specific actors"; and segmentalist states, such as Argentina, have a weak polity and a state that exists "outside society" as an external project (operating in the interests of a military or class elite). These differences in state structures and polities are argued to produce differences in the amount of formal organizing, the domains in which organizing will occur, the types of structures developing, and the "form of interpenetration of formal organizing with polity and society" (pp. 215-218). In short, Jepperson and Meyer argue that broad differences among types of organizations and organizational fields may be accounted for by systematic differences in the ways in which societies organize power and construct agency.[5]

The developing and testing of these types of variation-finding and encompassing arguments should be high on the agenda of institutional scholars.

Concluding Comment

Institutional theory has experienced a broad revival in the social sciences during the past two decades. Nowhere has its impact been greater than in the arena of organizational studies. In important respects, organizations came into existence as a specialized area of inquiry because theorists emphasized the distinctiveness of organizations as against other social collectivities. Early scholars pointed to the relative independence and insulation of organizations from their surroundings and to their rational structuring in the pursuit of specialized objectives. These distinctive features now appear to us as having been overstated.

Institutionalists remind us that no organization can be properly understood apart from its wider social and cultural context. These environments create the infrastructures—regulative, normative, and cognitive—that constrain and support the operation of individual organizations. The formal structures of organizations are seen, at least in part, to represent theories of action that embody the prevailing cultural logics. Rationalities are contextualized.

Current theory and research reflects existing confusion and controversies over what are the fundamental building blocks of institutions. Are the pillars of these structures bundles of sanctions, collections of norms, or clusters of cognitions? Do institutions vary in their reliance on one or another of these pillars? Do different institutional forms have different effects on the constituent units?

Other questions of importance are also raised. How do institutions arise and persist? decline and collapse? How are changes in institutional forms and processes related to changes in organizational forms and processes? These sorts of questions can only be answered if we broaden current research agendas. Social science remains overly parochial and pedestrian. We are too prone to select our study populations out of convenience rather than theoretical promise. In particular, we are too prone to study systems close to us in time and place. We do this in spite of the fact that these are the very systems that are most difficult to see with fresh eyes. These systems co-opt and corrupt our vision because we are likely to share many of our subjects' beliefs and assumptions. We need the frame-breaking experiences that only come from examining and comprehending organizations operating in other places and other times.

Notes

1. In addition to pressures stemming from institutionalists to take more account of history, ecologists have also contributed to making historical time and developmental processes more salient to the study of organizations.

2. It can be observed that the new institutionalists in sociology have changed their position over time regarding the relation between rationality and institutional behavior. In the early, founding statements, Meyer and Rowan (1977), DiMaggio and Powell (1983), and Tolbert and Zucker (1983) all embraced the view that institutional structures and forms were, if not irrational, at least nonrational in character. Institutional structures were viewed in contrast to structures driven by efficiency forces.

An intermediate position was proposed by Scott and Meyer (1983/1991) in which institutional and "technical" (efficiency) forces are seen as orthogonal and varying in strength. Organizations can be subject to (1) strong technical forces coupled with weak institutional forces, (2) the reverse situation, (3) simultaneously to strong institutional and strong technical forces, or (4) simultaneously to weak forces of each type. This argument assumes that institutional and rational forces may be alternative sources of structure and behavior but that they are not necessarily in conflict.

The more recent neo-institutional position among sociologists, just described, is that institutional forces encompass and subsume rational ones. The rules of rationality are set by institutional processes and vary from one institution to another. This position has been embraced by Scott (1987), Fligstein (1990), Friedland and Alford (1991), and Powell (1991), among others.

3. For a special journal issue devoted to longitudinal field research methods for studying organizational processes, see Van de Ven and Huber (1990).

4. Although Fligstein gives some attention to variation finding—factors causing differences among corporations in their tendency to adopt similar forms—he gives more emphasis to factors conducing all corporations to adopt a common form.

5. For a study that comes close to developing an encompassing framework, see the research by Hamilton, Biggart, and colleagues (Hamilton and Biggart 1988; Orru et al. 1991). They examine differences among Japan, South Korea, and Taiwan in their state structures, market economies, and technological development as these affect the organization of business groups within each society.

References

Abbott, Andrew. 1988. *The System of Professions: An Essay on the Division of Expert Labor.* Chicago: University of Chicago Press.

———. 1990. "A Primer on Sequence Methods." *Organization Science* 1:375-392.

———. 1992. "An Old Institutionalist Reads the New Institutionalism." *Contemporary Sociology* 21:754-756.

Abell, Peter. Forthcoming. "The New Institutionalism and Rational Choice Theory." In *The Institutional Construction of Organizations,* edited by W. Richard Scott and Søren Christensen. Thousand Oaks, CA: Sage.

Abrahamson, Eric. 1991. "Managerial Fads and Fashions: The Diffusion and Rejection of Innovations." *Academy of Management Review* 16:586-612.

Abrahamson, Eric and Charles J. Fombrun. 1994. "Macro-Cultures: Determinants and Consequences." *Academy of Management Review* 19:728-755.

Abzug, Rikki and Stephen J. Mezias. 1993. "The Fragmented State and Due Process Protections in Organizations: The Case of Comparable Worth." *Organization Science* 4:433-453.

Alchian, Armen A. and Harold Demsetz. 1972. "Production, Information Costs, and Economic Organization." *American Economic Review* 62:777-795.

Aldrich, Howard E. and C. Marlene Fiol. 1994. "Fools Rush In? The Institutional Context of Industry Creation." *Academy of Management Review* 19:645-670.

Alexander, Jeffrey A. and Thomas A. D'Aunno. 1990. "Transformation of Institutional Environments: Perspectives on the Corporatization of U.S. Health Care." Pp. 53-85 in *Innovations in Health Care Delivery: Insights for Organization Theory,* edited by Stephen S. Mick. San Francisco: Jossey-Bass.

Alexander, Jeffrey C. 1983a. *Theoretical Logic in Sociology: The Antinomies of Classical Thought: Marx and Durkheim.* Vol. 2. Berkeley: University of California Press.

————. 1983b. *Theoretical Logic in Sociology: The Classical Attempt at Theorical Synthesis: Max Weber.* Vol. 3. Berkeley: University of California Press.

————. 1983c. *Theoretical Logic in Sociology: The Modern Reconstruction of Classical Thought: Talcott Parsons.* Vol. 4. Berkeley: University of California Press.

Armour, H. O. and David Teece. 1978. "Organizational Structure and Economic Performance." *Bell Journal of Economics* 9:106-122.

Aronowitz, Stanley. 1992. *The Politics of Identity: Class, Culture and Social Movements.* New York: Routledge, Chapman and Hall.

Arthur, W. Brian. 1988. "Self-Reinforcing Mechanisms in Economics." Pp. 9-32 in *The Economy as an Evolving Complex System,* edited by P. W. Anderson and Kenneth J. Arrow. Menlo Park, CA: Addison-Wesley.

Ashforth, Blake E. and Barrie W. Gibbs. 1990. "The Double-Edge of Organizational Legitimation." *Organization Science* 1:177-194.

Axelrod, Robert. 1984. *The Evolution of Cooperation.* New York: Basic Books.

Barley, Stephen R. 1986. "Technology as an Occasion for Structuring: Evidence From Observations of CT Scanners and the Social Order of Radiology Departments." *Administrative Science Quarterly* 31:78-108.

Barley, Stephen R. and Gideon Kunda. 1992. "Design and Devotion: Surges of Rational and Normative Ideologies of Control in Managerial Discourse." *Administrative Science Quarterly* 37:363-399.

Barnard, Chester I. 1938. *The Functions of the Executive.* Cambridge, MA: Harvard University Press.

Barnett, William P. and Glenn R. Carroll. 1993a. "How Institutional Constraints Affected the Organization of Early U.S. Telephony." *Journal of Law, Economics and Organization* 9:98-126.

————. 1993b. "Organizational Ecology Approaches to Institutions." Pp. 171-181 in *Interdisciplinary Perspectives on Organization Studies,* edited by Siegwart M. Lindenberg and Hein Schreuder. Oxford, UK: Pergamon.

Baron, James N., Frank R. Dobbin, and P. Deveraux Jennings. 1986. "War and Peace: The Evolution of Modern Personnel Administration in U.S. Industry." *American Journal of Sociology* 92:350-383.

Bartunek, J. M. 1984. "Changing Interpretive Schemes and Organizational Restructuring: The Example of a Religious Order." *Administrative Science Quarterly* 29:355-372.

Baum, Joel A. C. and Christine Oliver. 1991. "Institutional Linkages and Organizational Mortality." *Administrative Science Quarterly* 36:187-218.

————. 1992. "Institutional Imbeddedness and the Dynamics of Organizational Populations." *American Sociological Review* 57:540-559.

Baum, Joel A. C. and Jitendra V. Singh, eds. 1994. *Evolutionary Dynamics of Organizations.* New York: Oxford University Press.

Becker, Howard S. 1982. *Art Worlds.* Berkeley: University of California Press.

Bendix, Reinhard. 1960. *Max Weber: An Intellectual Portrait.* Garden City, NY: Doubleday.

Berger, Peter L., Brigitte Berger, and Hansfried Kellner. 1973. *The Homeless Mind: Modernization and Consciousness.* New York: Random House.

Berger, Peter L. and Hansfried Kellner. 1981. *Sociology Interpreted: An Essay on Method and Vocation.* Garden City, NY: Doubleday Anchor.

Berger, Peter L. and Thomas Luckmann. 1967. *The Social Construction of Reality.* New York: Doubleday Anchor.

Biggart, Nicole Woolsey and Gary G. Hamilton. 1992. "On the Limits of a Firm-Based Theory to Explain Business Networks: The Western Bias of Neoclassical Economics." Pp. 471-490 in *Networks and Organizations: Structure, Form, and Action,* edited by Nitin Nohria and Robert G. Eccles. Boston: Harvard Business School Press.

Bijker, Wiebe, Thomas P. Hughes, and Trevor Pinch, eds. 1987. *The Social Construction of Techno-logical Systems: New Directions in the Sociology and History of Technology.* Cambridge: MIT Press.

Bill, James A. and Robert L. Hardgrave, Jr. 1981. *Comparative Politics: The Quest for Theory.* Washington, DC: Bell & Howell, University Press of America.

Blau, Peter M. 1955. *The Dynamics of Bureaucracy.* Chicago: University of Chicago Press.

Blau, Peter M. and W. Richard Scott. 1962. *Formal Organizations: A Comparative Approach.* San Francisco: Chandler.

Boeker, Warren P. 1988. "Organizational Origins: Entrepreneurial and Environmental Imprinting at the Time of Founding." Pp. 33-51 in *Ecological Models of Organizations,* edited by Glenn R. Carroll. Cambridge, MA: Ballinger.

———. 1989. "The Development and Institutionalization of Subunit Power in Organizations." *Administrative Science Quarterly* 34:388-410.

Bourdieu, Pierre. 1975. "The Specificity of the Scientific Field and the Social Conditions for the Progress of Reason." *Social Science Information* 14(6):19-47.

———. 1977. *Outline of a Theory of Practice.* Cambridge, UK: Cambridge University Press.

———. 1988. *Homo Academicus.* Stanford, CA: Stanford University Press.

———. 1990. *The Logic of Practice.* Stanford, CA: Stanford University Press.

Bourdieu, Pierre and Loic J. D. Wacquant. 1992. *An Invitation to Reflexive Sociology.* Chicago: University of Chicago Press.

Brint, Steven and Jerome Karabel. 1991. "Institutional Origins and Transformations: The Case of American Community Colleges." Pp. 337-360 in *The New Institutionalism in Organizational Analysis,* edited by Walter W. Powell and Paul J. DiMaggio. Chicago: University of Chicago Press.

Brown, Lawrence A. 1981. *Innovation Diffusion: A New Perspective.* London: Methuen.

Brunsson, Nils. 1989. *The Organization of Hypocrisy: Talk, Decisions and Actions in Organizations.* New York: John Wiley.

Buchanan, James M. and Gordon Tullock. 1962. *The Calculus of Consent.* Ann Arbor: University of Michigan Press.

Burawoy, Michael. 1979. *Manufacturing Consent: Changes in the Labor Process Under Monopoly Capitalism.* Chicago: University of Chicago Press.

———. 1985. *The Politics of Production: Factory Regimes Under Capitalism and Socialism.* London: Verso.

Burgess, John William. 1902. *Political Science and Comparative Constitutional Law.* Boston: Ginn.

Burke, Peter J. and Donald C. Reitzes. 1981. "The Link Between Identity and Role Performance." *Social Psychology Quarterly* 44:83-92.

———. 1991. "An Identity Theory Approach to Commitment." *Social Psychology Quarterly* 54:239-251.

Burns, Lawton R. and Douglas R. Wholey. 1993. "Adoption and Abandonment of Matrix Management Programs: Effects of Organizational Characteristics and Interorganizational Networks." *Academy of Management Journal* 36:106-138.

Burrell, Gibson and Gareth Morgan. 1979. *Sociological Paradigms and Organisational Analysis.* London: Heinemann.

Burt, Ronald S. 1987. "Social Contagion and Innovation: Cohesion Versus Structural Equivalence." *American Journal of Sociology* 92:1287-1335.

Calhoun, Craig. 1990. "Introduction: Toward a Sociology of Business." Pp. 1-17 in *Comparative Social Research: Business Institutions,* edited by Craig Calhoun. Vol. 12. Greenwich, CT: JAI.

———. 1991. "The Problem of Identity in Collective Action." Pp. 51-75 in *Macro-Micro Linkages in Sociology,* edited by Joan Huber. Newbury Park, CA: Sage.

Camic, Charles. 1992. "Reputation and Predecessor Selection: Parsons and the Institutionalists." *American Sociological Review* 57:421-445.

Campbell, John L., J. Rogers Hollingsworth, and Leon N. Lindberg, eds. 1991. *Governance of the American Economy.* New York: Cambridge University Press.

Campbell, John L. and Leon N. Lindberg. 1990. "Property Rights and the Organization of Economic Activity by the State." *American Sociological Review* 55:634-647.

———. 1991. "The Evolution of Governance Regimes." Pp. 319-355 in *Governance of the American Economy,* edited by John L. Campbell, J. Rogers Hollingsworth, and Leon N. Lindberg. New York: Cambridge University Press.

Carroll, Glenn R. 1984. "Organizational Ecology." *Annual Review of Sociology* 10:71-93.

———. 1987. *Publish and Perish: The Organizational Ecology of Newspaper Industries.* Greenwich, CT: JAI.

Carroll, Glenn R. and Jacques Delacroix. 1982. "Organizational Mortality in the Newspaper Industries of Argentina and Ireland: An Ecological Approach." *Administrative Science Quarterly* 27:169-198.

Carroll, Glenn R., Jacques Delacroix, and Jerry Goodstein. 1988. "The Political Environments of Organizations: An Ecological View." Pp. 359-392 in *Research in Organizational Behavior,* edited by Barry M. Staw and L. L. Cummings. Vol. 10. Greenwich, CT: JAI.

Carroll, Glenn R., Jerry Goodstein, and Antal Gyenes. 1988. "Organizations and the State: Effects of the Institutional Environment on Agricultural Cooperatives in Hungary." *Administrative Science Quarterly* 33:233-256.

Carroll, Glenn R. and Michael T. Hannan. 1989. "Density Dependence in the Evolution of Populations of Newspaper Organizations." *American Sociological Review* 54:524-548.

Carroll, Glenn R. and Yangchung Paul Huo. 1986. "Organizational Task and Institutional Environments in Ecological Perspective: Findings From the Local Newspaper Industry." *American Journal of Sociology* 91:838-873.

Cawson, Alan, ed. 1985. *Organized Interests and the State: Studies in Meso-Corporatism.* Beverly Hills, CA: Sage.

Chandler, Alfred D., Jr. 1962. *Strategy and Structure: Chapters in the History of the American Industrial Enterprise.* Cambridge: MIT Press.

———. 1977. *The Visible Hand: The Managerial Revolution in American Business.* Cambridge, MA: Belknap Press of Harvard University Press.

Chin, Robert and Kenneth D. Benne. 1976. "General Strategies for Effecting Changes in Human Systems." Pp. 22-45 in *The Planning of Change,* edited by Warren G. Bennis, Kenneth D. Benne, Robert Chin, and Kenneth E. Correy. 3rd ed. New York: Holt, Rinehart and Winston.

Clark, Burton R. 1960. *The Open Door College.* New York: McGraw-Hill.

———. 1970. *The Distinctive College: Antioch, Reed, and Swarthmore.* Chicago: Aldine.

Coase, Ronald H. 1937. "The Nature of the Firm." *Economica* 4:385-405.

———. 1972. "Industrial Organization: A Proposal for Research." Pp. 59-73 in *Policy Issues and Research Opportunities in Industrial Organization,* edited by Victor R. Fuchs. New York: National Bureau of Economic Research.

———. 1983. "The New Institutional Economics." *Journal of Institutional and Theoretical Economics* 140:229-231.

Cole, Robert E. 1989. *Strategies for Learning: Small-Group Activities in American, Japanese, and Swedish Industry.* Berkeley: University of California Press.

Coleman, James R. 1974. *Power and the Structure of Society.* New York: Norton.

———. 1990. *Foundations of Social Theory.* Cambridge, MA: Belknap Press of Harvard University Press.

Commons, John R. 1924. *The Legal Foundations of Capitalism.* New York: Macmillan.

———. 1970. *The Economics of Collective Action.* Madison: University of Wisconsin Press. (Original work published 1950)

Cooley, Charles Horton. 1956. *Social Organization*. Glencoe, IL: Free Press. (Original work published 1902)

Covaleski, Mark A. and Mark W. Dirsmith. 1988. "An Institutional Perspective on the Rise, Social Transformation and Fall of a University Budget Category." *Administrative Science Quarterly* 33:562-587.

Creighton, Andrew L. 1990. "The Emergence of Incorporation as a Legal Form for Organizations." Unpublished doctoral dissertation, Department of Sociology, Stanford University, Stanford, CA.

D'Andrade, Roy G. 1984. "Cultural Meaning Systems." Pp. 88-119 in *Culture Theory: Essays on Mind, Self, and Emotion*, edited by Richard A. Shweder and Robert A. LeVine. Cambridge, UK: Cambridge University Press.

D'Aunno, Thomas, Robert I. Sutton, and Richard H. Price. 1991. "Isomorphism and External Support in Conflicting Institutional Environments: A Study of Drug Abuse Treatment Units." *Academy of Management Journal* 14:636-661.

David, Paul A. 1988. *Path-Dependence: Putting the Past Into the Future of Economics*. Institute for Mathematical Studies in the Social Sciences Technical Report No. 533, Stanford University, Stanford, CA.

———. 1992. "Why Are Institutions the 'Carriers of History'? Notes on Path-Dependence and the Evolution of Conventions, Organizations and Institutions." Paper presented to the Stanford Institute for Theoretical Economics, Stanford University, Stanford, CA, July.

Davis, Gerald F. 1991. "Agents Without Principles? The Spread of the Poison Pill Through the Intercorporate Network." *Administrative Science Quarterly* 36:583-613.

Delacroix, Jacques and Hayagreeva Rao. 1994. "Externalities and Ecological Theory: Unbundling Density Dependence." Pp. 255-268 in *Evolutionary Dynamics of Organizations*, edited by Joel A. C. Baum and Jitendra V. Singh. New York: Oxford University Press.

DiMaggio, Paul J. 1983. "State Expansion and Organization Fields." Pp. 147-161 in *Organization Theory and Public Policy*, edited by Richard H. Hall and Robert E. Quinn. Beverly Hills, CA: Sage.

———. 1986. "Structural Analysis of Organizational Fields: A Blockmodel Approach." Pp. 355-370 in *Research in Organization Behavior*, edited by Barry M. Staw and L. L. Cummings. Vol. 8. Greenwich, CT: JAI.

———. 1988. "Interest and Agency in Institutional Theory." Pp. 3-21 in *Institutional Patterns and Organizations: Culture and Environment*, edited by Lynne G. Zucker. Cambridge, MA: Ballinger.

———. 1991. "Constructing an Organizational Field as a Professional Project: U.S. Art Museums, 1920-1940." Pp. 267-292 in *The New Institutionalism in Organizational Analysis*, edited by Walter W. Powell and Paul J. DiMaggio. Chicago: University of Chicago Press.

DiMaggio, Paul J. and Walter W. Powell. 1983. "The Iron Cage Revisited: Institutional Isomorphism and Collective Rationality in Organizational Fields." *American Sociological Review* 48:147-160.

———. 1991. "Introduction." Pp. 1-38 in *The New Institutionalism in Organizational Analysis*, edited by Walter W. Powell and Paul J. DiMaggio. Chicago: University of Chicago Press.

Dobbin, Frank R. 1994. *Forging Industrial Policy: The United States, Britain, and France in the Railway Age*. New York: Cambridge University Press.

Dobbin, Frank R., Lauren Edelman, John W. Meyer, W. Richard Scott, and Ann Swidler. 1988. "The Expansion of Due Process in Organizations." Pp. 71-100 in *Institutional Patterns and Organizations: Culture and Environment*, edited by Lynne G. Zucker. Cambridge, MA: Ballinger.

Dobbin, Frank R., John R. Sutton, John W. Meyer, and W. Richard Scott. 1993. "Equal Opportunity Law and the Construction of Internal Labor Markets." *American Journal of Sociology* 99:396-427.

Dornbusch, Sanford M. and W. Richard Scott, with the assistance of Bruce C. Busching and James D. Laing. 1975. *Evaluation and the Exercise of Authority.* San Francisco: Jossey-Bass.

Douglas, Mary. 1986. *How Institutions Think.* Syracuse, NY: Syracuse University Press.

Durkheim, Émile. 1949. *The Division of Labor in Society.* Glencoe, IL: Free Press. (Original work published 1893)

———. 1950. *The Rules of Sociological Method.* Glencoe, IL: Free Press. (Original work published 1901)

———. 1961. *The Elementary Forms of Religious Life.* New York: Collier. (Original work published 1912)

Easton, David. 1965. *A Framework for Political Analysis.* Englewood Cliffs, NJ: Prentice Hall.

Eckstein, Harry. 1963. "A Perspective on Comparative Politics, Past and Present." Pp. 3-32 in *Comparative Politics,* edited by Harry Eckstein and David E. Apter. New York: Free Press of Glencoe.

Edelman, Lauren. 1990. "Legal Environments and Organizational Governance: The Expansion of Due Process in the American Workplace." *American Journal of Sociology* 95:1401-1440.

———. 1992. "Legal Ambiguity and Symbolic Structures: Organizational Mediation of Civil Rights Law." *American Journal of Sociology* 97:1531-1576.

Ellul, Jacques. 1964. *The Technological Society.* New York: Alfred A. Knopf. (Original work published 1954)

Elsbach, Kimberly D. and Robert I. Sutton. 1992. "Acquiring Organizational Legitimacy Through Illegitimate Actions: A Marriage of Institutional and Impression Management Theories." *Academy of Management Journal* 35:699-738.

Elster, Jon. 1983. *Explaining Technical Change: A Case Study in the Philosophy of Science.* Cambridge, UK: Cambridge University Press.

Evans, Peter B., Dietrich Rueschemeyer, and Theda Skocpol, eds. 1985. *Bringing the State Back In.* Cambridge, UK: Cambridge University Press.

Fennell, Mary L. and Jeffrey A. Alexander. 1993. "Perspectives on Organizational Change in the US Medical Care Sector." *Annual Review of Sociology* 19:89-112.

Fligstein, Neil. 1985. "The Spread of the Multidivisional Form Among Large Firms, 1919-1979." *American Sociological Review* 50:377-391.

———. 1987. "The Intraorganizational Power Struggle: The Rise of Finance Presidents in Large Corporations, 1919-1979." *American Sociological Review* 52:44-58.

———. 1990. *The Transformation of Corporate Control.* Cambridge, MA: Harvard University Press.

———. 1991. "The Structural Transformation of American Industry: An Institutional Account of the Causes of Diversification in the Largest Firms, 1919-1979." Pp. 311-336 in *The New Institutionalism in Organizational Analysis,* edited by Walter W. Powell and Paul J. DiMaggio. Chicago: University of Chicago Press.

Flood, Ann Barry and W. Richard Scott. 1987. *Hospital Structure and Performance.* Baltimore, MD: Johns Hopkins University Press.

Freidson, Eliot. 1970. *Profession of Medicine.* New York: Dodd, Mead.

———. 1986. *Professional Powers: A Study of the Institutionalization of Formal Knowledge.* Chicago: University of Chicago Press.

Friedland, Roger and Robert R. Alford. 1991. "Bringing Society Back In: Symbols, Practices, and Institutional Contradictions." Pp. 232-263 in *The New Institutionalism in Organizational Analysis,* edited by Walter W. Powell and Paul J. DiMaggio. Chicago: University of Chicago Press.

Fromm, Gary, ed. 1981. *Studies in Public Regulation.* Cambridge: MIT Press.

Frost, Peter, Larry F. Moore, Meryl Reis Louis, Craig C. Lundberg, and Joanne Martin. 1991. *Reframing Organizational Culture.* Newbury Park, CA: Sage.

Galaskiewicz, Joseph and Ronald S. Burt. 1991. "Interorganizational Contagion in Corporate Philanthropy." *Administrative Science Quarterly* 36:88-105.

Geertz, Clifford. 1973. *The Interpretation of Cultures*. New York: Basic Books.

Georgopoulos, Basil S. 1972. "The Hospital as an Organization and Problem-Solving System." Pp. 9-48 in *Organization Research on Health Institutions*, edited by Basil S. Georgopoulos. Ann Arbor: Institute for Social Research, University of Michigan.

Gergen, Kenneth J. and Keith E. Davis, eds. 1985. *The Social Construction of the Person*. New York: Springer-Verlag.

Giddens, Anthony. 1979. *Central Problems in Social Theory: Action, Structure and Contradiction in Social Analysis*. Berkeley: University of California Press.

―――. 1984. *The Constitution of Society*. Berkeley: University of California Press.

Glassman, Robert. 1973. "Persistence and Loose Coupling in Living Systems." *Behavioral Science* 18:83-98.

Goffman, Erving. 1961. *Asylums*. Garden City, NY: Doubleday, Anchor Books.

―――. 1974. *Frame Analysis*. Cambridge, MA: Harvard University Press.

Gonos, George. 1977. "Situation Versus Frame: The Interactionist and Structuralist Analysis of Everyday Life." *American Sociological Review* 42:854-867.

Goodstein, Jerry D. 1994. "Institutional Pressures and Strategic Responsiveness: Employer Involvement in Work-Family Issues." *Academy of Management Journal* 37:350-382.

Gouldner, Alvin W. 1954. *Patterns of Industrial Bureaucracy*. Glencoe, IL: Free Press.

Granovetter, Mark. 1985. "Economic Action and Social Structure: The Problem of Embeddedness." *American Journal of Sociology* 91:481-510.

Gray, Bradford H., ed. 1986. *For Profit Enterprise in Health Care*. Washington, DC: National Academy Press.

Greening, Daniel W. and Barbara Gray. 1994. "Testing a Model of Organizational Response to Social and Political Issues." *Academy of Management Journal* 37:467-498.

Gulick, Luther and L. Urwick, eds. 1937. *Papers in the Science of Administration*. New York: Institute of Public Administration, Columbia University.

Gusfield, Joseph R. 1955. "Social Structure and Moral Reform: A Study of the Women's Christian Temperance Union." *American Journal of Sociology* 61:221-232.

Hall, Peter A. 1986. *Governing the Economy: The Politics of State Intervention in Britain and France*. Cambridge, UK: Polity Press.

―――. 1992. "The Movement From Keynesianism to Monetarism: Institutional Analysis and British Economic Policy in the 1970s." Pp. 90-113 in *Structuring Politics: Historical Institutionalism in Comparative Analysis*, edited by Sven Steinmo, Kathleen Thelen, and Frank Longstreth. Cambridge, UK: Cambridge University Press.

Hall, Richard H. 1992. "Taking Things a Bit Too Far: Same Problems With Emergent Institutional Theory." Pp. 71-87 in *Issues, Theory and Research in Industrial Organizational Psychology*, edited by Kathryn Kelley. Amsterdam, The Netherlands: Elsevier.

Halliday, Terence C., Michael J. Powell, and Mark W. Granfors. 1993. "After Minimalism: Transformation of State Bar Associations From Market Dependence to State Reliance, 1918 to 1950." *American Sociological Review* 58:515-535.

Hamilton, Gary and Nicole W. Biggart. 1988. "Market, Culture, and Authority: A Comparative Analysis of Management and Organization in the Far East." *American Journal of Sociology* 94(Supplement):S52-S94.

Hannan, Michael T. and Glenn Carroll. 1992. *Dynamics of Organizational Populations: Density, Legitimation, and Competition*. New York: Oxford University Press.

Hannan, Michael T. and John Freeman. 1977. "The Population Ecology of Organizations." *American Journal of Sociology* 82:929-964.

————. 1984. "Structural Inertia and Organizational Change." *American Sociological Review* 49:149-164.

————. 1989. *Organizational Ecology.* Cambridge, MA: Harvard University Press.

Haunschild, Pamela R. 1993. "Interorganizational Imitation: The Impact of Interlocks on Corporate Acquisition Activity." *Administrative Science Quarterly* 38:564-592.

Haveman, Heather A. 1993. "Follow the Leader: Mimetic Isomorphism and Entry Into New Markets." *Administrative Science Quarterly* 38:593-627.

Hay, Peter. 1993. "Royal Treatment." *Performing Arts.* March, p. 70.

Hechter, Michael. 1987. *Principles of Group Solidarity.* Berkeley: University of California Press.

————. 1990. "The Emergence of Cooperative Social Institutions." Pp. 13-33 in *Social Institutions: Their Emergence, Maintenance, and Effects,* edited by Michael Hechter, Karl-Dieter Opp, and Reinhard Wippler. New York: Aldine de Gruyter.

Hechter, Michael, Karl-Dieter Opp, and Reinhard Wippler, eds. 1990. *Social Institutions: Their Emergence, Maintenance, and Effects.* New York: Aldine de Gruyter.

Hemenway, David. 1975. *Industrywide Voluntary Product Standards.* Cambridge, MA: Ballinger.

Hirsch, Paul M. 1985. "The Study of Industries." Pp. 271-309 in *Research in the Sociology of Organizations,* edited by Samuel B. Bacharach and Stephen M. Mitchell. Vol. 4. Greenwich, CT: JAI.

————. 1986. "From Ambushes to Golden Parachutes: Corporate Takeovers as an Instance of Cultural Framing and Institutional Integration." *American Journal of Sociology* 91:800-837.

Hodgson, Geoffrey. 1988. *Economics and Institutions: A Manifesto for a Modern Institutional Economics.* Philadelphia: University of Pennsylvania Press.

————. 1991. "Institutional Economic Theory: The Old Versus the New." Pp. 194-213 in *After Marx and Sraffa: Essays in Political Economy,* by Geoffrey M. Hodgson. New York: St. Martin's.

Horowitz, Donald L. 1979. "The Courts as Monitors of the Bureaucracy." Pp. 89-102 in *Making Bureaucracies Work,* edited by Carol H. Weiss and Allen H. Barton. Beverly Hills, CA: Sage.

Hughes, Everett C. 1936. "The Ecological Aspect of Institutions." *American Sociological Review* 1:180-189.

————. 1939. "Institutions." Pp. 281-330 in *An Outline of the Principles of Sociology,* edited by Robert E. Park. New York: Barnes & Noble.

————. 1958. *Men and Their Work.* Glencoe, IL: Free Press. (Collected essays dating from 1928)

Hult, Karen M. and Charles Walcott. 1990. *Governing Public Organizations: Politics, Structures, and Institutional Design.* Pacific Grove, CA: Brooks/Cole.

Jaccoby, Sanford M. 1988. "What Can Economics Learn From Industrial Relations?" Unpublished paper, Anderson Graduate School of Management, University of California, Los Angeles.

————. 1990. "The New Institutionalism: What Can It Learn From the Old?" *Industrial Relations* 29:316-359.

Jensen, Michael C. and William H. Meckling. 1976. "Theory of the Firm: Managerial Behavior, Agency Costs, and Ownership Structure." *Journal of Financial Economics* 3:305-360.

Jepperson, Ronald L. 1991. "Institutions, Institutional Effects, and Institutionalization." Pp. 143-163 in *The New Institutionalism in Organizational Analysis,* edited by Walter W. Powell and Paul J. DiMaggio. Chicago: University of Chicago Press.

Jepperson, Ronald L. and John W. Meyer. 1991. "The Public Order and the Construction of Formal Organizations." Pp. 204-231 in *The New Institutionalism in Organizational Analysis,* edited by Walter W. Powell and Paul J. DiMaggio. Chicago: University of Chicago Press.

Jones, Edward E. and Keith E. Davis. 1965. "From Acts to Dispositions: The Attribution Process in Person Perception." Pp. 220-266 in *Advances in Experimental Social Psychology,* edited by Leonard Berkowitz. Vol. 2. New York: Academic Press.

Kanter, Rosabeth Moss. 1977. *Men and Women of the Corporation.* New York: Basic Books.

Kaplan, Marilyn R. and J. Richard Harrison. 1993. "Defusing the Director Liability Crisis: The Strategic Management of Legal Threats." *Organization Science* 4:412-432.

Katz, Daniel and Robert L. Kahn. 1978. *The Social Psychology of Organizations.* 2nd ed. New York: John Wiley.

Kilduff, Martin. 1993. "The Reproduction of Inertia in Multinational Corporations." Pp. 259-274 in *Organization Theory and the Multinational Corporation,* edited by Sumantra Ghoshal and D. Eleanor Westney. New York: St. Martin's.

Kimberly, John R. 1975. "Environmental Constraints and Organizational Structure: A Comparative Analysis of Rehabilitation Organizations." *Administrative Science Quarterly* 20:1-9.

Kiser, Edgar and Michael Hechter. 1991. "The Role of General Theory in Comparative-Historical Sociology." *American Journal of Sociology* 97:1-30.

Kitschelt, Herbert. 1991. "Industrial Governance Structures, Innovation Strategies, and the Case of Japan: Sectoral or Cross-National Comparative Analysis?" *International Organization* 45:453-493.

Knoke, David. 1982. "The Spread of Municipal Reform: Temporal, Spatial, and Social Dynamics." *American Journal of Sociology* 87:1314-1339.

Knudsen, Christian. 1993. "Modelling Rationality, Institutions and Processes in Economic Theory." Pp. 265-299 in *Rationality, Institutions, and Economic Methodology,* edited by Uskali Maki, Bo Gustafsson, and Christian Knudsen. London: Routledge.

Krasner, Stephen D., ed. 1983. *International Regimes.* Ithaca, NY: Cornell University Press.

———. 1988. "Sovereignty: An Institutional Perspective." *Comparative Political Studies* 21:66-94.

Langlois, Richard N. 1986a. "The New Institutional Economics: An Introductory Essay." Pp. 1-25 in *Economics as a Process: Essays in the New Institutional Economics.* New York: Cambridge University Press.

———. 1986b. "Rationality, Institutions, and Explanations." Pp. 225-255 in *Economics as a Process: Essays in the New Institutional Economics,* edited by Richard N. Langlois. New York: Cambridge University Press.

Lant, Theresa K. and Joel A. C. Baum. Forthcoming. "Cognitive Sources of Socially Constructed Competitive Groups: Examples From the Manhattan Hotel Industry." In *The Institutional Construction of Organizations,* edited by W. Richard Scott and Søren Christensen. Thousand Oaks, CA: Sage.

Lasswell, Harold. 1936. *Politics: Who Gets What, When, How?* New York: Whittlesey House.

Laumann, Edward O. and David Knoke. 1987. *The Organizational State: Social Choice in National Policy Domains.* Madison: University of Wisconsin Press.

Lave, Charles A. and James G. March. 1975. *An Introduction to Models in the Social Sciences.* New York: Harper & Row.

Leblebici, Husayin and Gerald R. Salancik. 1982. "Stability in Interorganizational Exchanges: Rulemaking Processes of the Chicago Board of Trade." *Administrative Science Quarterly* 27:227-242.

Leblebici, Husayin, Gerald R. Salancik, Anne Copay, and Tom King. 1991. "Institutional Change and the Transformation of Interorganizational Fields: An Organizational History of the U.S. Radio Broadcasting Industry." *Administrative Science Quarterly* 36:333-363.

Lewin, Kurt. 1951. *Field Theory in Social Psychology.* New York: Harper.

Lincoln, James R. 1990. "Japanese Organization and Organization Theory." Pp. 256-293 in *Research in Organizational Behavior,* edited by Barry M. Staw and L. L. Cummings. Vol. 12. Greenwich, CT: JAI.

Lindblom, Charles E. 1977. *Politics and Markets: The World's Political-Economic Systems.* New York: Basic Books.

Lipset, Seymour Martin, Martin A. Trow, and James S. Coleman. 1956. *Union Democracy.* Glencoe, IL: Free Press.

Lord, Robert G. and Mary C. Kernan. 1987. "Scripts as Determinants of Purposeful Behavior in Organizations." *Academy of Management Review* 12:265-277.

Macaulay, Stewart. 1963. "Non-Contractual Relations in Business." *American Sociological Review.* 28:55-70.

Maines, David R. 1977. "Social Organization and Social Structure in Symbolic Interactionist Thought." *Annual Review of Sociology* 3:235-259.

March, James G., ed. 1965. *Handbook of Organizations.* Chicago: Rand McNally.

———. 1981. "Decisions in Organizations and Theories of Choice." Pp. 205-244 in *Perspectives on Organization Design and Behavior,* edited by Andrew H. Van de Ven and William F. Joyce. New York: John Wiley, Wiley-Interscience.

———. 1994. *A Primer on Decision Making: How Decisions Happen.* New York: Free Press.

March, James G. and Johan P. Olsen. 1984. "The New Institutionalism: Organizational Factors in Political Life." *American Political Science Review* 78:734-749.

———. 1989. *Rediscovering Institutions: The Organizational Basis of Politics.* New York: Free Press.

March, James G. and Herbert A. Simon. 1958. *Organizations.* New York: John Wiley.

Mares, David R. and Walter W. Powell. 1990. "Cooperative Security Regimes: Preventing International Conflicts." Pp. 55-94 in *Organizations and Nation-States: New Perspectives on Conflict and Cooperation,* edited by Robert L. Kahn and Mayer N. Zald. San Francisco: Jossey-Bass.

Markus, Hazel and R. B. Zajonc. 1985. "The Cognitive Perspective in Social Psychology." Pp. 137-230 in *Handbook of Social Psychology,* edited by Gardner Lindzey and Elliot Aronson. Vol. 1, 3rd ed. New York: Random House.

Martin, Joanne. 1994. "The Organization of Exclusion: The Institutionalization of Sex Inequality, Gendered Faculty Jobs, and Gendered Knowledge in Organizational Theory and Research." *Organizations* 1:401-431.

Mead, George Herbert. 1934. *Mind, Self and Society.* Chicago: University of Chicago Press.

Menger, Carl. 1963. *Problems of Economics and Sociology.* Translated by F. J. Nock. Urbana: University of Illinois Press. (Original work published 1871)

Merton, Robert K. 1936. "The Unanticipated Consequences of Purposive Social Action." *American Sociological Review* 1:894-904.

———. 1957. "Bureaucratic Structure and Personality." Pp. 195-206 in *Social Theory and Social Structure,* by Robert K. Merton. 2nd ed. Glencoe, IL: Free Press. (Original work published 1940)

Merton, Robert K., Ailsa P. Gray, Barbara Hockey, and Hanan C. Selvin, eds. 1952. *Reader in Bureaucracy.* Glencoe, IL: Free Press.

Meyer, John W. 1983. "Conclusion: Institutionalization and the Rationality of Formal Organizational Structure." Pp. 261-282 in *Organizational Environments: Ritual and Rationality,* edited by John W. Meyer and W. Richard Scott. Beverly Hills, CA: Sage.

———. 1994. "Rationalized Environments." Pp. 28-54 in *Institutional Environments and Organizations: Structural Complexity and Individualism,* edited by W. Richard Scott and John W. Meyer. Thousand Oaks, CA: Sage.

Meyer, John W., John Boli, and George M. Thomas. 1987. "Ontology and Rationalization in the Western Cultural Account." Pp. 12-37 in *Institutional Structure: Constituting State, Society, and the Individual,* edited by George M. Thomas, John W. Meyer, Francisco O. Ramirez, and John Boli. Newbury Park, CA: Sage.

Meyer, John W. and Michael T. Hannan. 1979. *National Development and the World System.* Chicago: University of Chicago Press.

Meyer, John W., David Kamens, Aaron Benavot, Y. K. Cha, and S. Y. Wong. 1992. *School Knowledge for the Masses: World Models and National Primary Curriculum Categories in the Twentieth Century.* London: Falmer.

Meyer, John W. and Brian Rowan. 1977. "Institutionalized Organizations: Formal Structure as Myth and Ceremony." *American Journal of Sociology* 83:340-363.

Meyer, John W. and W. Richard Scott. 1983a. "Centralization and the Legitimacy Problems of Local Government." Pp. 199-215 in *Organizational Environments: Ritual and Rationality,* edited by John W. Meyer and W. Richard Scott. Beverly Hills, CA: Sage.

Meyer, John W. and W. Richard Scott, with the assistance of Brian Rowan and Terrence E. Deal. 1983b. *Organizational Environments: Ritual and Rationality.* Beverly Hills, CA: Sage. (Updated edition in 1992)

Meyer, John W., W. Richard Scott, and Terrence E. Deal. 1981. "Institutional and Technical Sources of Organizational Structure: Explaining the Structure of Educational Organizations." Pp. 151-178 in *Organization and the Human Services,* edited by Herman D. Stein. Philadelphia, PA: Temple University Press.

Meyer, John W., W. Richard Scott, and David Strang. 1987. "Centralization, Fragmentation, and School District Complexity." *Administrative Science Quarterly* 32:186-201.

Meyer, John W., W. Richard Scott, David Strang, and Andrew L. Creighton. 1988. "Bureaucratization Without Centralization: Changes in the Organizational System of U.S. Public Education, 1940-80." Pp. 139-168 in *Institutional Patterns and Organizations: Culture and Environment,* edited by Lynne G. Zucker. Cambridge, MA: Ballinger.

Mezias, Stephen J. 1990. "An Institutional Model of Organizational Practice: Financial Reporting at the Fortune 200." *Administrative Science Quarterly* 35:431-457.

Miles, Robert H. 1982. *Coffin Nails and Corporate Strategy.* Englewood Cliffs, NJ: Prentice Hall.

Miller, Jon. 1994. *The Social Control of Religious Zeal: A Study of Organizational Contradictions.* New Brunswick, NJ: Rutgers University Press.

Moe, Terry M. 1984. "The New Economics of Organization." *American Journal of Political Science* 28:739-777.

————. 1990a. "Political Institutions: The Neglected Side of the Story." *Journal of Law, Economics and Organizations* 6:213-253.

————. 1990b. "The Politics of Structural Choice: Toward a Theory of Public Bureaucracy." Pp. 116-153 in *Organization Theory: From Chester Barnard to the Present and Beyond,* edited by Oliver E. Williamson. New York: Oxford University Press.

Mohr, Lawrence B. 1982. *Explaining Organizational Behavior.* San Francisco: Jossey-Bass.

Murphree, Mary C. 1987. "New Technology and Office Tradition: The Not-So-Changing World of the Secretary." Pp. 98-135 in *Computer Chips and Paper Clips: Technology and Women's Employment. Vol. II: Case Studies and Policy Perspectives,* edited by Heidi I. Hartmann. Washington, DC: National Academy Press.

Neisser, U. 1976. *Cognition and Reality: Principles and Implications of Cognitive Psychology.* San Francisco: Freeman.

Nelson, Richard R. 1986. "The Tension Between Process Stories and Equilibrium Models: Analyzing the Productivity-Growth Slowdown of the 1970s." Pp. 135-151 in *Economics as a Process: Essays in the New Institutional Economics,* edited by Richard N. Langlois. Cambridge, UK: Cambridge University Press.

Nelson, Richard R. and Sidney G. Winter. 1982. *An Evolutionary Theory of Economic Change.* Cambridge, MA: Belknap Press of Harvard University Press.

Nisbett, Richard and Lee Ross. 1980. *Human Inference: Strategies and Shortcomings of Social Judgment.* Englewood Cliffs, NJ: Prentice Hall.

Noll, Roger T., ed. 1985. *Regulatory Policy and the Social Sciences.* Berkeley: University of California Press.

North, Douglass C. 1990. *Institutions, Institutional Change and Economic Performance.* Cambridge, UK: Cambridge University Press.

North, Douglass C. and Robert Paul Thomas. 1973. *The Rise of the Western World: A New Economic History.* Cambridge, UK: Cambridge University Press.

Oliver, Christine. 1991. "Strategic Responses to Institutional Processes." *Academy of Management Review* 16:145-179.

————. 1992. "The Antecedents of Deinstitutionalization." *Organization Studies* 13:563-588.

Orlikowski, Wanda A. 1992. "The Duality of Technology: Rethinking the Concept of Technology in Organizations." *Organization Science* 3:398-427.

Orru, Marco, Nicole Woolsey Biggart, and Gary G. Hamilton. 1991. "Organizational Isomorphism in East Asia." Pp. 361-389 in *The New Institutionalism in Organizational Analysis,* edited by Walter W. Powell and Paul J. DiMaggio. Chicago: University of Chicago Press.

Orton, J. Douglas and Karl E. Weick. 1990. "Loosely Coupled Systems: A Reconceptualization." *Academy of Management Review* 15:203-223.

Parsons, Talcott. 1937. *The Structure of Social Action.* New York: McGraw-Hill.

————. 1951. *The Social System.* New York: Free Press.

————. 1953. "A Revised Analytical Approach to the Theory of Social Stratification." Pp. 92-129 in *Class, Status and Power: A Reader in Social Stratification,* edited by Reinhard Bendix and Seymour M. Lipset. Glencoe, IL: Free Press.

————. 1960a. "A Sociological Approach to the Theory of Organizations." Pp. 16-58 in *Structure and Process in Modern Societies,* by Talcott Parsons. Glencoe, IL: Free Press. (Original work published 1956)

————. 1960b. "Some Ingredients of a General Theory of Formal Organization." Pp. 59-96 in *Structure and Process in Modern Societies,* by Talcott Parsons. Glencoe, IL: Free Press. (Original work published 1956)

————. 1990. "Prolegomena to a Theory of Social Institutions." *American Sociological Review* 55:319-339. (Original work written 1934)

Perrow, Charles. 1961. "The Analysis of Goals in Complex Organizations." *American Sociological Review* 26:854-866.

————. 1986. *Complex Organizations: A Critical Essay.* 3rd ed. New York: Random House.

Peters, B. Guy. 1988. "The Machinery of Government." Pp. 19-53 in *Organizing Governance; Governing Organizations,* edited by Colin Campbell and B. Guy Peters. Pittsburgh, PA: University of Pittsburgh Press.

Peterson, Paul E., Barry G. Rabe, and Kenneth K. Wong. 1986. *When Federalism Works.* Washington, DC: Brookings Institution.

Pfeffer, Jeffrey and Gerald Salancik. 1978. *The External Control of Organizations.* New York: Harper & Row.

Porac, Joe and H. Thomas. 1990. "Taxonomic Mental Models in Competitor Definition." *Academy of Management Review* 15:224-240.

Porac, Joe, H. Thomas, and C. Badden-Fuller. 1989. "Competitive Groups as Cognitive Communities: The Case of the Scottish Knitwear Manufacturers." *Journal of Management Studies* 26:397-415.

Powell, Walter W. 1988. "Institutional Effects on Organizational Structure and Performance." Pp. 115-136 in *Institutional Patterns and Organizations: Culture and Environment,* edited by Lynne G. Zucker. Cambridge, MA: Ballinger.

————. 1991. "Expanding the Scope of Institutional Analysis." Pp. 183-203 in *The New Institutionalism in Organizational Analysis,* edited by Walter W. Powell and Paul J. DiMaggio. Chicago: University of Chicago Press.

Powell, Walter W. and Paul J. DiMaggio, eds. 1991. *The New Institutionalism in Organizational Analysis.* Chicago: University of Chicago Press.

Pratt, John W. and Richard J. Zeckhauser, eds. 1985. *Principals and Agents: The Structure of Business.* Boston, MA: Harvard Business School Press.

President's Research Committee on Social Trends. 1933. *Recent Social Trends in the United States.* New York: McGraw-Hill.

Rabinow, Paul and William M. Sullivan, eds. 1987. *Interpretive Social Science: A Second Look.* Berkeley: University of California Press.

Ranger-Moore, James, Jane Banaszak-Holl, and Michael T. Hannan. 1991. "Density-Dependent Dynamics in Regulated Industries: Founding Rates of Banks and Life Insurance Companies." *Administrative Science Quarterly* 36:36-65.

Reed, Michael. 1985. *Redirections in Organizational Analysis.* London: Tavistock.

Roethlisberger, Fritz J. and William J. Dickson. 1939. *Management and the Worker.* Cambridge, MA: Harvard University Press.

Rosenau, Pauline Marie. 1991. *Post-Modernism and the Social Sciences: Insights, Inroads, and Intrusions.* Princeton, NJ: Princeton University Press.

Rosenberg, Morris. 1979. *Conceiving the Self.* New York: Basic Books.

Rosenkopf, Lori and Michael L. Tushman. 1994. "The Coevolution of Technology and Organization." Pp. 403-424 in *Evolutionary Dynamics of Organizations,* edited by Joel A. C. Baum and Jitendra V. Singh. New York: Oxford University Press.

Rowan, Brian. 1982. "Organizational Structure and the Institutional Environment: The Case of Public Schools." *Administrative Science Quarterly* 27:196-198.

Roy, Donald. 1952. "Quota Restriction and Goldbricking in a Machine Shop." *American Journal of Sociology* 57:427-442.

Rumelt, Richard. 1974. *Strategy, Structure and Economic Performance.* Boston, MA: Harvard Business School Press.

Salaman, Graeme. 1978. "Toward a Sociology of Organisational Structure." *Sociological Review* 26:519-554.

Schank, R. C. and R. P. Abelson. 1977. *Scripts, Plans, Goals, and Understanding.* Hillsdale, NJ: Lawrence Erlbaum.

Schmoller, Gustav von. 1900-1904. *Grundriss der Allgemeinen Volkswirtschaftslehre [Fundamentals of General Economic Principles].* Leipzig, Germany: Duncker & Humblot.

Schotter, Andrew. 1981. *The Economic Theory of Social Institutions.* New York: Cambridge University Press.

———. 1986. "The Evolution of Rules." Pp. 117-134 in *Economics as a Process: Essays in the New Institutional Economics,* edited by Richard N. Langlois. New York: Cambridge University Press.

Schmitter, Philippe. 1990. "Sectors in Modern Capitalism: Models of Governance and Variations in Performance." Pp. 3-39 in *Labour Relations and Economic Performance,* edited by Renato Brunetta and Carlo Dell'Aringa. Houndmills, England: Macmillan.

Schrödinger, Erwin. 1945. *What Is Life?* New York: Cambridge University Press.

Schumpeter, Joseph A. 1961. *The Theory of Economic Development.* New York: Oxford University Press.

Schutz, Alfred. 1962. *Collected Papers.* Edited by Maurice Natanson. The Hague, The Netherlands: Nijhoff.

Scott, W. Richard. 1977. "The Effectiveness of Organizational Effectiveness Studies." Pp. 63-95 in *New Perspectives on Organizational Effectiveness,* edited by Paul S. Goodman and Johannes M. Pennings. San Francisco: Jossey-Bass.

———. 1983. "The Organization of Environments: Network, Cultural, and Historical Elements." Pp. 155-175 in *Organizational Environments: Ritual and Rationality,* edited by John W. Meyer and W. Richard Scott. Beverly Hills, CA: Sage.

————. 1987. "The Adolescence of Institutional Theory." *Administrative Science Quarterly* 32:493-511.

————. 1991. "The Evolution of Organization Theory." Pp. 53-68 in *Studies in Organizational Sociology: Essays in Honor of Charles K. Warriner,* edited by Gale Miller. Greenwich, CT: JAI.

————. 1992. *Organizations: Rational, Natural and Open Systems.* 3rd ed. Englewood Cliffs, NJ: Prentice Hall.

————. 1993. "The Organization of Medical Care Services: Toward an Integrated Theoretical Model." *Medical Care Review* 59:271-302.

————. 1994a. "Conceptualizing Organizational Fields: Linking Organizations and Societal Systems." Pp. 203-221 in *Systemrationalität und Partialinteresse* [Systems Rationality and Partial Interests], edited by Hans-Ulrich Derlien, Uta Gerhardt, and Fritz W. Scharpf. Baden-Baden, Germany: Nomos Verlagsgesellschaft.

————. 1994b. "Institutional Analysis: Variance and Process Theory Approaches." Pp. 81-99 in *Institutional Environments and Organizations: Structural Complexity and Individualism,* edited by W. Richard Scott and John W. Meyer. Thousand Oaks, CA: Sage.

————. 1994c. "Institutions and Organizations: Toward a Theoretical Synthesis." Pp. 55-80 in *Institutional Environments and Organizations: Structural Complexity and Individualism,* edited by W. Richard Scott and John W. Meyer. Thousand Oaks, CA: Sage.

————. 1994d. "Law and Organizations." Pp. 3-18 in *The Legalistic Organization,* edited by Sim B. Sitkin and Robert J. Bies. Thousand Oaks, CA: Sage.

Scott, W. Richard and Elaine V. Backman. 1990. "Institutional Theory and the Medical Care Sector." Pp. 20-52 in *Innovations in Health Care Delivery: Insights for Organization Theory,* edited by Stephen S. Mick. San Francisco: Jossey-Bass.

Scott, W. Richard and John W. Meyer. 1983. "The Organization of Societal Sectors." Pp. 129-153 in *Organizational Environments: Ritual and Rationality,* edited by John W. Meyer and W. Richard Scott. (Revised version pp. 108-140 in *The New Institutionalism in Organizational Analysis,* edited by Walter W. Powell and Paul J. DiMaggio. Chicago: University of Chicago Press, 1991)

————. 1988. "Environmental Linkages and Organizational Complexity: Public and Private Schools." Pp. 128-160 in *Comparing Public and Private Schools: Vol. 1: Institutions and Organizations,* edited by Tom James and Henry M. Levin. Philadelphia, PA: Falmer.

————. 1991. "The Rise of Training Programs in Firms and Agencies: An Institutional Perspective." Pp. 297-326 in *Research in Organization Behavior,* edited by Barry M. Staw and L. L. Cummings. Vol. 13. Greenwich, CT: JAI.

————, eds. 1994. *Institutional Environments and Organizations: Structural Complexity and Individualism.* Thousand Oaks, CA: Sage.

Searing, Donald D. 1991. "Roles, Rules, and Rationality in the New Institutionalism." *American Political Science Review* 85:1239-1260.

Searle, John R. 1969. *Speech Acts: An Essay in the Philosophy of Language.* Cambridge, UK: Cambridge University Press.

Seavoy, Ronald E. 1982. *The Origins of the American Business Corporation, 1784-1855: Broadening the Concept of Public Service During Industrialization.* Westport, CT: Greenwood.

Selznick, Philip. 1948. "Foundations of the Theory of Organization." *American Sociological Review* 13:25-35.

————. 1949. *TVA and the Grass Roots.* Berkeley: University of California Press.

————. 1957. *Leadership in Administration.* New York: Harper & Row.

Shepsle, Kenneth A. and Barry Weingast. 1987. "The Institutional Foundations of Committee Power." *American Political Science Review* 81:85-104.

Shortell, Stephen M., Ellen Morrison, and S. L. Hughes. 1990. *Strategic Choices for America's Hospitals: Managing Change in Turbulent Times.* San Francisco: Jossey-Bass.

Silverman, David. 1971. *The Theory of Organizations: A Sociological Framework.* New York: Basic Books.

———. 1972. "Some Neglected Questions About Social Reality." Pp. 165-182 in *New Directions in Sociological Theory,* by Paul Filmer, Michael Phillipson, David Silverman, and David Walsh. Cambridge: MIT Press.

Silverman, David and J. Jones. 1976. *Organisational Work: The Language of Grading and the Grading of Language.* London: Macmillan.

Simon, Herbert A. 1957. *Administrative Behavior.* 2nd ed. New York: Macmillan. (Original work published 1945)

———. 1991. *Models of My Life.* New York: Basic Books.

Singh, Jitendra V. 1993. "Review Essay: Density Dependence Theory—Current Issues, Future Promise." *American Journal of Sociology* 99:464-473.

Singh, Jitendra V. and Charles J. Lumsden. 1990. "Theory and Research in Organizational Ecology." *Annual Review of Sociology* 16:161-195.

Singh, Jitendra V., David J. Tucker, and Robert J. House. 1986. "Organizational Legitimacy and the Liability of Newness." *Administrative Science Quarterly* 31:171-193.

Skocpol, Theda. 1979. *States and Social Revolutions.* Cambridge, UK: Cambridge University Press.

———. 1984. "Emerging Agendas and Recurrent Strategies in Historical Sociology." Pp. 356-391 in *Vision and Method in Historical Sociology,* edited by Theda Skocpol. Cambridge, UK: Cambridge University Press.

———. 1985. "Bringing the State Back In: Strategies of Analysis in Current Research." Pp. 3-37 in *Bringing the State Back In,* edited by Peter B. Evans, Dietrich Rueschemeyer, and Theda Skocpol. Cambridge, UK: Cambridge University Press.

———. 1992. *Protecting Soldiers and Mothers: The Political Origins of Social Policy in the United States.* Cambridge, MA: Harvard University Press.

Skowronek, Stephen. 1982. *Building a New American State: The Expansion of National Administrative Capacities, 1877-1920.* Cambridge, UK: Cambridge University Press.

Somers, Margaret R. and Gloria D. Gibson. Forthcoming. "Reclaiming the Epistemological Other: Narrative and the Social Constitution of Identity." In *From Persons to Nations: The Social Constitution of Identities,* edited by Craig Calhoun. London: Basil Blackwell.

Starr, Paul. 1982. *The Social Transformation of American Medicine.* New York: Basic Books.

Stern, Robert N. 1979. "The Development of an Interorganizational Control Network: The Case of Intercollegiate Athletics." *Administrative Science Quarterly* 24:242-266.

Stigler, George J. 1968. *The Organization of Industry.* Homewood, IL: Irwin.

Stinchcombe, Arthur L. 1965. "Social Structure and Organizations." Pp. 142-193 in *Handbook of Organizations,* edited by James G. March. Chicago: Rand McNally.

———. 1968. *Constructing Social Theories.* Chicago: University of Chicago Press.

Strang, David and John W. Meyer. 1993. "Institutional Conditions for Diffusion." *Theory and Society* 22:487-511.

Streeck, Wolfgang and Philippe C. Schmitter. 1985a. "Community, Market, State—and Associations? The Prospective Contribution of Interest Governance to Social Order." Pp. 1-29 in *Private Interest Government: Beyond Market and State,* edited by Wolfgang Streeck and Philippe C. Schmitter. Beverly Hills, CA: Sage.

———, eds. 1985b. *Private Interest Government: Beyond Market and State.* Beverly Hills, CA: Sage.

Stryker, Sheldon. 1980. *Symbolic Interactionism: A Social Structural Version.* Menlo Park, CA: Cummings.

Stubbart, C. I. and A. Ramaprasad. 1988. "Probing Two Chief Executives' Schematic Knowledge of the U.S. Steel Industry Using Cognitive Maps." Pp. 139-164 in *Advances in Strategic Management,* edited by R. Lamb and P. Shrivastava. Vol. 5. Greenwich, CT: JAI.

Suchman, Mark C. 1994. "On Advice of Counsel: Legal and Financial Firms as Information Intermediaries in the Structuration of Silicon Valley." Unpublished doctoral dissertation, Department of Sociology, Stanford University, Stanford, CA.

———. Forthcoming. "Localism and Globalism in Institutional Analysis: The Emergence of Contractual Norms in Venture Finance." In *The Institutional Construction of Organizations: International and Longitudinal Studies,* edited by W. Richard Scott and Søren Christensen. Thousand Oaks, CA: Sage.

Sugden, Robert. 1986. *The Economics of Rights, Cooperation and Welfare.* Oxford, UK: Basil Blackwell.

Sutton, John R., Frank R. Dobbin, John W. Meyer, and W. Richard Scott. 1994. "The Legalization of the Workplace." *American Journal of Sociology* 99:944-971.

Swedberg, Richard. 1991. "Major Traditions of Economic Sociology." *Annual Review of Sociology* 17:251-276.

Swidler, Ann. 1986. "Culture in Action: Symbols and Strategies." *American Sociological Review* 51:273-286.

Takata, Azumi Ann. 1994. "From Merchant House to Corporation: The Development of the Modern Corporate Form and the Transformation of Business Organization in Japan, 1853-1912." Unpublished doctoral dissertation, Department of Sociology, Stanford University, Stanford, CA.

Taylor, Serge. 1984. *Making Bureaucracies Think: The Environmental Impact Statement Strategy of Administrative Reform.* Stanford, CA: Stanford University Press.

Teece, David J. 1981. "Internal Organization and Economic Performance: An Empirical Study of the Profitability of Principal Firms." *Journal of Industrial Economics* 30(December):173-200.

Thelen, Kathleen and Sven Steinmo. 1992. "Historical Institutionalism in Comparative Politics." In *Structuring Politics: Historical Institutionalism in Comparative Analysis,* edited by Sven Steinmo, Kathleen Thelen, and Frank Longstreth. Cambridge, UK: Cambridge University Press.

Thomas, George M. and John W. Meyer. 1984. "The Expansion of the State." *Annual Review of Sociology* 10:461-482.

Thomas, George M., John W. Meyer, Francisco O. Ramirez, and John Boli, eds. 1987. *Institutional Structure: Constituting State, Society, and the Individual.* Newbury Park, CA: Sage.

Tilly, Charles. 1984. *Big Structures, Large Processes, Huge Comparisons.* New York: Russell Sage.

Thompson, James D. 1967. *Organizations in Action.* New York: McGraw-Hill.

Tolbert, Pamela S. and Lynne G. Zucker. 1983. "Institutional Sources of Change in the Formal Structure of Organizations: The Diffusion of Civil Service Reform, 1880-1935." *Administrative Science Quarterly* 30:22-39.

Tullock, Gordon. 1976. *The Vote Motive.* London: Institute for Economic Affairs.

Tuma, Nancy B. and Michael T. Hannan. 1984. *Social Dynamics: Models and Methods.* New York: Academic Press.

Tuma, Nancy B., Michael T. Hannan, and Lyle P. Groeneveld. 1979. "Dynamic Analysis of Event Histories." *American Journal of Sociology* 26:187-206.

Turner, Roy, ed. 1974. *Ethnomethodology: Selected Readings.* Harmondsworth, UK: Penguin.

Tushman, Michael L. and Philip Anderson. 1986. "Technological Discontinuities and Organizational Environments." *Administrative Science Quarterly* 31:439-465.

Tversky, Amos and Donald Kahneman. 1974. "Judgment Under Uncertainty." *Science* 185:1124-1131.

Van de Ven, Andrew H. 1992. "Suggestions for Studying Strategy Process." *Strategic Management Journal* 13:169-188.

Vanberg, Viktor. 1989. "Carl Menger's Evolutionary and John R. Commons' Collective Action Approach to Institutions: A Comparison." *Review of Political Economy* 1:334-360.

———. 1993. "The Institutional Theory of John R. Commons: A Review and Commentary." *Academy of Management Review* 18:129-152.

Van de Ven, Andrew H. and Raghu Garud. 1989. "A Framework for Understanding the Emergence of New Industries." Pp. 195-225 in *Research on Technological Innovation, Management and Policy*, edited by Richard S. Rosenbloom. Greenwich, CT: JAI.

———. 1994. "The Coevolution of Technical and Institutional Events in the Development of an Innovation." Pp. 425-443 in *Evolutionary Dynamics of Organizations*, edited by Joel A. C. Baum and Jitendra Singh. New York: Oxford University Press.

Van de Ven, Andrew H. and George P. Huber, eds. 1990. "Longitudinal Field Research Methods for Studying Processes of Organizational Change." *Organization Science* 1(3):213-335 and (4):375-439. (Special Issues)

Veblen, Thorstein B. 1898. "Why Is Economics Not an Evolutionary Science?" *Quarterly Journal of Economics* 12:373-397.

———. 1909. "The Limitations of Marginal Utility." *Journal of Political Economy* 17:235-245.

———. 1919. *The Place of Science in Modern Civilisation and Other Essays*. New York: Huebsch.

Walker, Gordon and David Weber. 1984. "A Transaction Cost Approach to Make-or-Buy Decisions." *Administrative Science Quarterly* 29:373-391.

Wallerstein, Immanuel. 1979. "From Feudalism to Capitalism: Transition or Transitions." Pp. 138-151 in *The Capitalist World-Economy: Essays by Immanuel Wallerstein*. Cambridge, UK: Cambridge University Press.

Weber, Max. 1946. *From Max Weber: Essays in Sociology*. Translated and edited by Hans H. Gerth and C. Wright Mills. New York: Oxford University Press. (Original essays published 1906-1924)

———. 1947. *The Theory of Social and Economic Organization*. Translated and edited by A. M. Henderson and Talcott Parsons. New York: Oxford University Press. (Original work published 1924)

———. 1949. *The Methodology of the Social Sciences*. Translated and edited by Edward A. Shils and Henry A. Finch. Glencoe, IL: Free Press. (Original essays published 1904-1918)

———. 1968. *Economy and Society: An Interpretive Sociology*. 3 vols. Edited by Guenther Roth and Claus Wittich. New York: Bedminister. (Original work published 1924)

Weick, Karl E. 1976. "Educational Organizations as Loosely Coupled Systems." *Administrative Science Quarterly* 21:1-19.

———. 1979. *The Social Psychology of Organizing*. 2nd ed. Reading, MA: Addison-Wesley.

———. 1993. "Sensemaking in Organizations: Small Structures With Large Consequences." Pp. 10-37 in *Social Psychology in Organizations: Advances in Theory and Research*, edited by J. Keith Murnighan. Englewood Cliffs, NJ: Prentice Hall.

Weingast, Barry R. 1989. "The Political Institutions of Representative Government." *Working Papers in Political Science* P-89-14. Hoover Institution, Stanford University, Stanford, CA.

Westney, D. Eleanor. 1987. *Imitation and Innovation: The Transfer of Western Organizational Patterns to Meiji Japan*. Cambridge, MA: Harvard University Press.

———. 1993. "Institutional Theory and the Multinational Corporation." Pp. 53-76 in *Organization Theory and the Multinational Corporation*, edited by Sumantra Ghoshal and D. Eleanor Westney. New York: St. Martin's.

Westphal, James D. and Edward J. Zajac. 1994. "Substance and Symbolism in CEO's Long-Term Incentive Plans." *Administrative Science Quarterly* 39:367-390.

Whitley, Richard. 1992a. *Business Systems in East Asia: Firms, Markets and Societies*. London: Sage.

———. 1992b. "The Social Construction of Organizations and Markets: The Comparative Analysis of Business Recipes." Pp. 120-143 in *Rethinking Organizations: New Directions in Organization Theory and Analysis*, edited by Michael Reed and Michael Hughes. Newbury Park, CA: Sage.

———. 1992c. "Societies, Firms and Markets: The Social Structuring of Business Systems." Pp. 5-44 in *European Business Systems: Firms and Markets in Their National Contexts,* edited by Richard Whitley. London: Sage.

Wholey, Douglas R. and Susan M. Sanchez. 1991. "The Effects of Regulatory Tools on Organizational Populations." *Academy of Management Review* 16:743-767.

Wilks, Stephen and Maurice Wright, eds. 1987. *Comparative Government-Industry Relations.* Oxford: Clarendon.

Williamson, Oliver E. 1975. *Markets and Hierarchies: Analysis and Antitrust Implications.* New York: Free Press.

———. 1981. "The Economics of Organization: The Transaction Cost Approach." *American Journal of Sociology* 87:548-577.

———. 1985. *The Economic Institutions of Capitalism.* New York: Free Press.

———. 1991. "Comparative Economic Organization: The Analysis of Discrete Structural Alternatives." *Administrative Science Quarterly* 36:269-296.

———. 1992. "Transaction Cost Economics and Organization Theory." Unpublished paper, Haas School of Business Administration, University of California, Berkeley.

Willoughby, Westel Woodbury. 1896. *An Examination of the Nature of the State.* New York: Macmillan.

———. 1904. *The American Constitutional System.* New York: Century.

Wilson, James Q., ed. 1980. *The Politics of Regulation.* New York: Basic Books.

Wilson, Woodrow. 1889. *The State and Federal Governments of the United States.* Boston: D. C. Heath.

Winter, Sidney G. 1990. "Survival, Selection, and Inheritance in Evolutionary Theories of Organization." Pp. 269-297 in *Organizational Evolution: New Directions,* edited by Jitendra V. Singh. Newbury Park, CA: Sage.

Wuthnow, Robert, James D. Hunter, Albert J. Bergesen, and Edith Kurzwell. 1984. *Cultural Analysis: The Works of Peter L. Berger, Mary Douglas, Michel Foucault, and Jürgen Habermas.* Boston: Routledge & Kegan Paul.

Yarbrough, Beth V. and Robert M. Yarbrough. 1990. "International Institutions and the New Economics of Organization." *International Organization* 44:235-259.

Zald, Mayer N. 1990. "History, Sociology, and Theories of Organization." Pp. 81-108 in *Institutions in American Society: Essays in Market, Political and Social Organizations,* edited by John J. Jackson. Ann Arbor: University of Michigan Press.

———. 1993. "Organization Studies as a Scientific and Humanistic Enterprise: Toward a Reconceptualization of the Foundations of the Field." *Organization Science* 4:513-528.

Zald, Mayer N. and Patricia Denton. 1963. "From Evangelism to General Service: The Transformation of the YMCA." *Administrative Science Quarterly* 8:214-234.

Zhou, Xueguang. 1993. "Occupational Power, State Capacities, and the Diffusion of Licensing in the American States: 1890 to 1950." *American Sociological Review* 58:536-552.

Zimmerman, Donald. 1969. "Fact as a Practical Accomplishment." Pp. 128-143 in *Ethnomethodology,* edited by Roy Turner. Middlesex, UK: Penguin.

Zucker, Lynne G. 1977. "The Role of Institutionalization in Cultural Persistence." *American Sociological Review* 42:726-743.

———. 1987. "Institutional Theories of Organization." *Annual Review of Sociology* 13:443-464.

———, ed. 1988a. *Institutional Patterns and Organizations: Culture and Environment.* Cambridge, MA: Ballinger.

———. 1988b. "Where Do Institutional Patterns Come From? Organizations as Actors in Social Systems." Pp. 23-49 in *Institutional Patterns and Organizations: Culture and Environment,* edited by Lynne G. Zucker. Cambridge, MA: Ballinger.

————. 1989. "Combining Institutional Theory and Population Ecology: No Legitimacy, No History (Comment on Carroll-Hannan, 1989)." *American Sociological Review* 54:542-545.

————. 1991. "Postscript: Microfoundations of Institutional Thought." Pp. 103-106 in *The New Institutionalism in Organizational Analysis*, edited by Walter W. Powell and Paul J. DiMaggio. Chicago: University of Chicago Press.

Index

About the Author

W. Richard Scott is Professor in the Department of Sociology with courtesy appointments in the Graduate School of Business, the School of Education, and the School of Medicine at Stanford University. He also serves as the founding Director of the Stanford Center for Organizational Research.

Professor Scott is the author of two widely used textbooks in the field of organizations: the early book, *Formal Organizations* (1962), written with Peter M. Blau, and the more recent book, *Organizations: Rational, Natural and Open Systems* (1992), now in its third edition.

He has focused particularly on the study of professional organizations, including social work, educational, and medical care organizations. His publications on these topics include the books *Evaluation and the Exercise of Authority* (1975), with Sanford M. Dornbusch, and *Hospital Structure and Performance* (1987), with Ann Barry Flood. During the past 10 years, he has collaborated with John W. Meyer in a series of studies on how institutional structures shape organizations. Portions of this work are contained in two edited collections, Meyer and Scott, *Organizational Environments: Ritual and Rationality* (1983,

2nd ed., 1992) and Scott and Meyer, *Institutional Environments and Organizations: Structural Complexity and Individualism* (1994).

He is a past fellow of the Center for Advanced Study in the Behavioral Sciences and was the recipient in 1988 of the Distinguished Scholar Award from the Management and Organization Theory Division of the Academy of Management. He is a member of the Institute of Medicine in the National Academy of Sciences and currently serves as a member of the Commission on Behavioral and Social Sciences and Education of the National Research Council.